I0709587

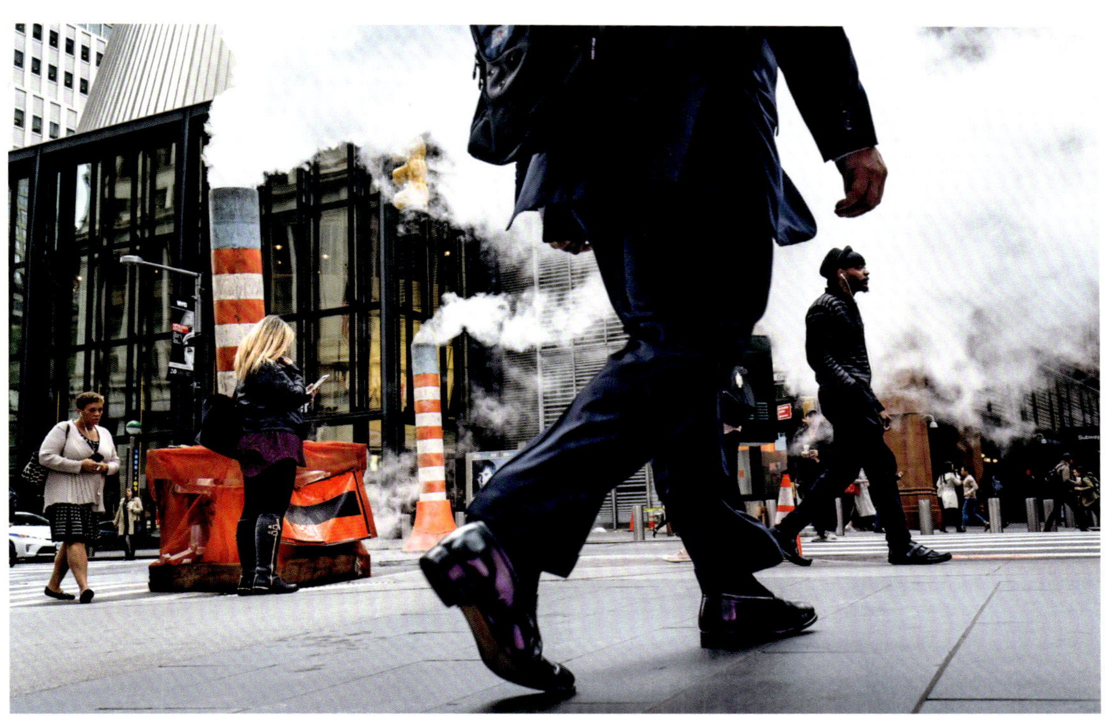

Cofounders: Taj Forer and Michael Itkoff
Creative Director: Ursula Damm
Copy Editor: Gabrielle Fastman

Quotes:
P. 20: Mary Ellen Mark, *Mary Ellen Mark on the Portrait and the Moment*.
    Aperture Foundation Books.
P. 39: Harry Gruyaert, Magnum Photos
P. 60: Jay Maisel
P. 76: Saul Leiter
P. 92: Ernst Haas
P. 107: Elliott Erwitt, Magnum Photos, *The Joy of Photographing People*, page 14.
    Eastman Kodak Company.

ISBN: 978-1-954119-27-7

Printed by Ofset Yapimevi, Turkey

Daylight Books
E-mail: info@daylightbooks.org
Web: www.daylightbooks.org

RELATIVE STRANGERS

TERI VERSHEL

For my children, Rachel & Leo,
for filling my heart with love and joy.

Always remember, it's never too late to
discover your passions.

FOREWORD

BY SAM ABELL

When I look at Teri Vershel's images, I hear music. It's the energetic, deliberately dissonant, and jazz-influenced first eleven minutes of George Gershwin's *Rhapsody in Blue*. These are the minutes that changed the direction of American music. They did so by being musically faithful to the reality of contemporary urban life.

The essence of that reality is the vibrant American street in all its clashing, colorful flow. Gershwin rendered that reality in music. Teri does it in her photographs.

Working in that realm puts Teri in another stream—the current of distinguished photographers who have taken street photography as their principal subject. Helen Levitt, Vivian Maier, Saul Leiter, Garry Winogrand, and Diane Arbus worked the American street for decades. Now Teri works it.

Like her predecessors, she does so because the street is seductive. For one thing, it's always there, calling to you. Step out the door and you're in step with street life. For Teri, that's more like a dance step. As a person and as a photographer she's in tune with the rhythm of the mingled, sometimes mangled, always honest choreography of the street. Like molecules, the visual elements of street life coalesce into meaningful moments, then dissolve, only to reform in another composition. Being in rhythm with these briefly occurring moments is the particular talent of street photographers like Teri.

But above all, the street, as a subject, is true. True to itself and to our time. It's fact, not fiction. The street is the opposite of studio work, where control is assured. This is reality street, where what you see is what you get—unless you're an astute observer like Teri. To her, the street is raw material to be distilled into images that give insight into the poetics of urban existence. The creative equation that begins with critical "street seeing" ends with a refined photograph and a new truth. Teri's truth.

An example is the complex, expressive photograph of a person striding into a city scene dominated by a cloud of steam and the corresponding strides of other pedestrians (page 1). It's a situation rich in potential.

But it isn't a photograph until Teri takes decisive action. She must see the situation evolving, sense its possibilities, and take action before the visual elements come together. That means quickly assuming a low stance to set the striding man against the steam while at the same time integrating the other pedestrians into the composition in a complementary way. It isn't easy. But the result is a meaningful, modern photograph.

Each of Teri's images can and should be read like this: as a stand-alone aesthetic experience. But the design of this book offers another intriguing opportunity. And that is to see individual images as one half of an arresting duet. By pairing Teri's images, new patterns—of content, color, texture, and graphics—emerge. The succession of these pairings builds into a fresh, original portrait of street life.

It is altogether fitting that Teri's work emerges now, exactly 100 years since Gershwin wrote and first performed *Rhapsody in Blue*. Across time, space, and genres, Teri's work, like Gershwin's, speaks to the timeless but ever-renewing music—and meaning—of the American street.

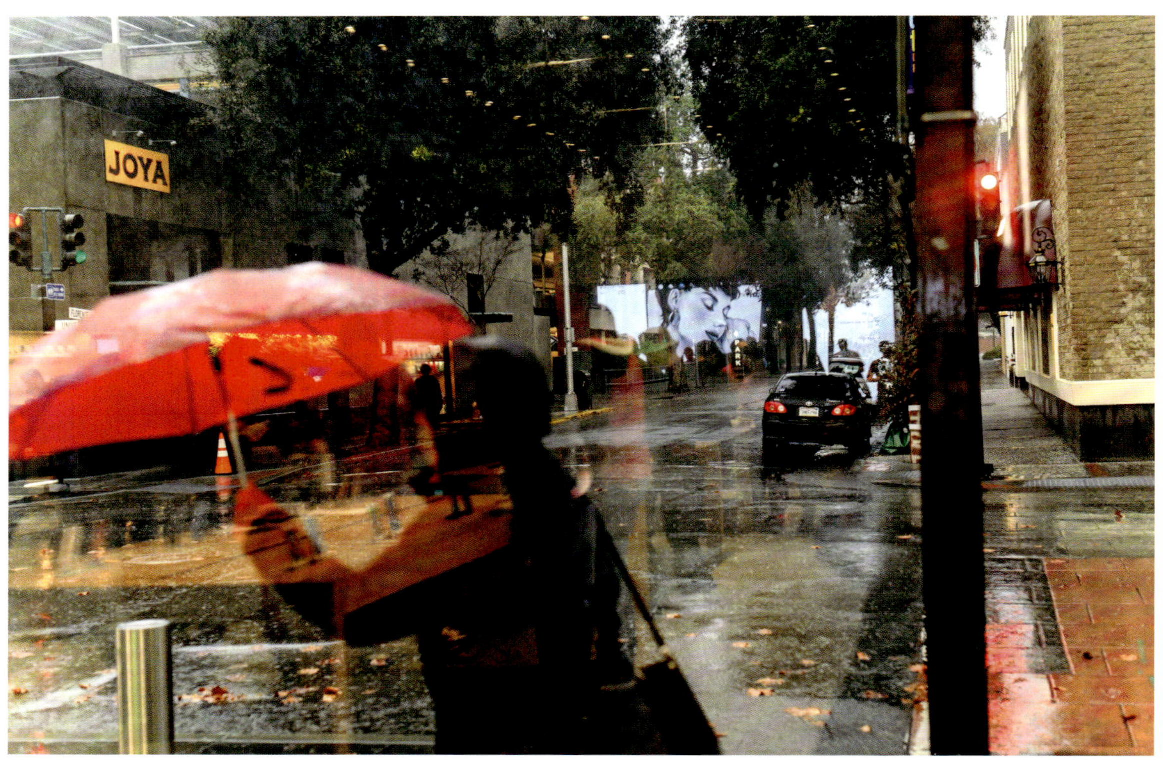
JOYA

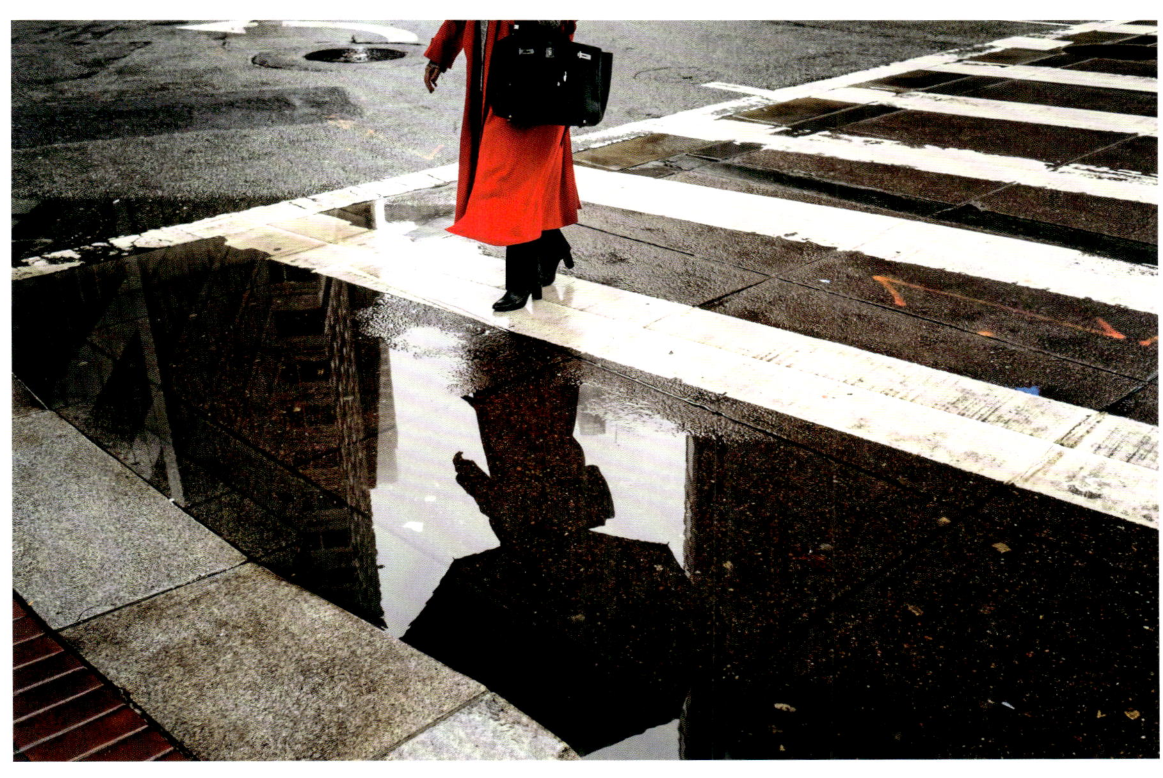

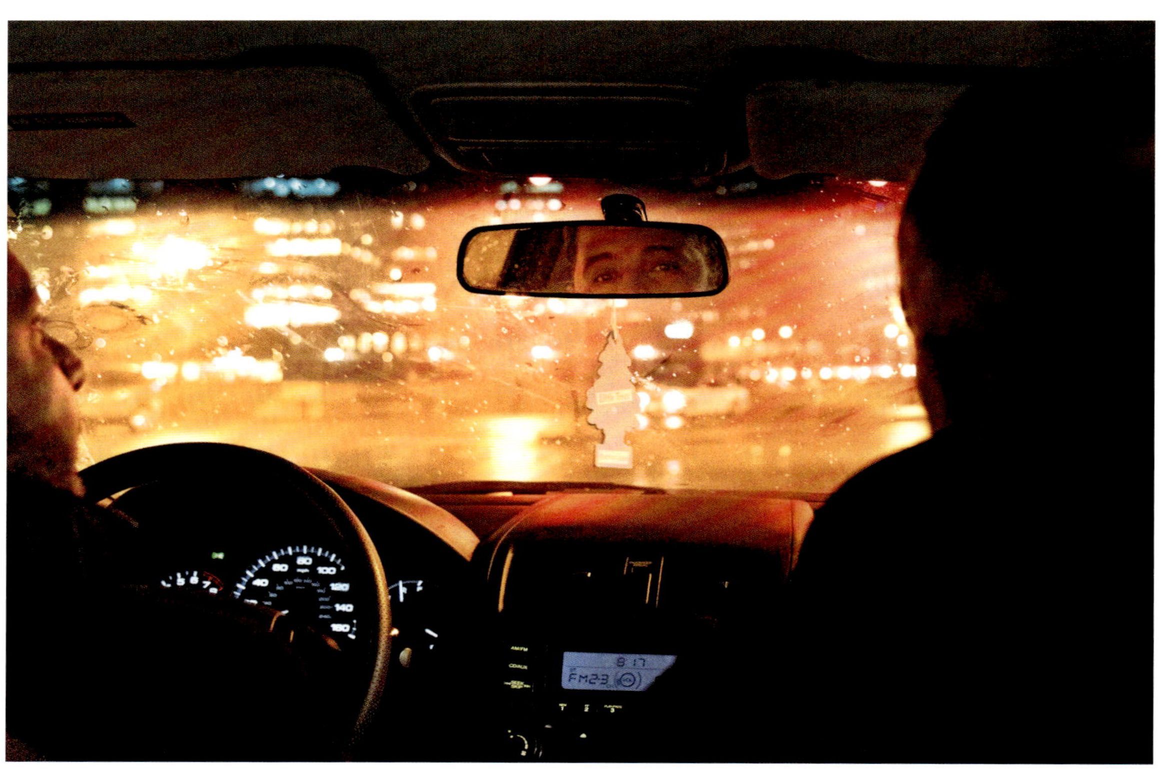

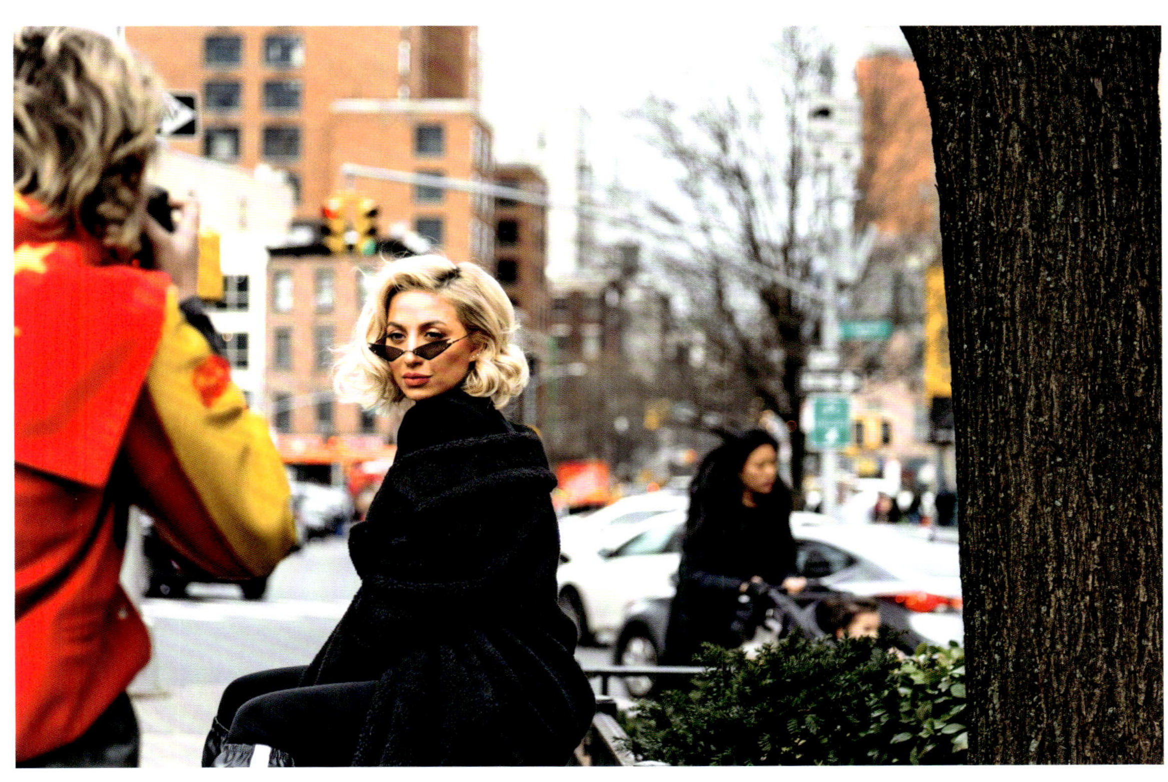

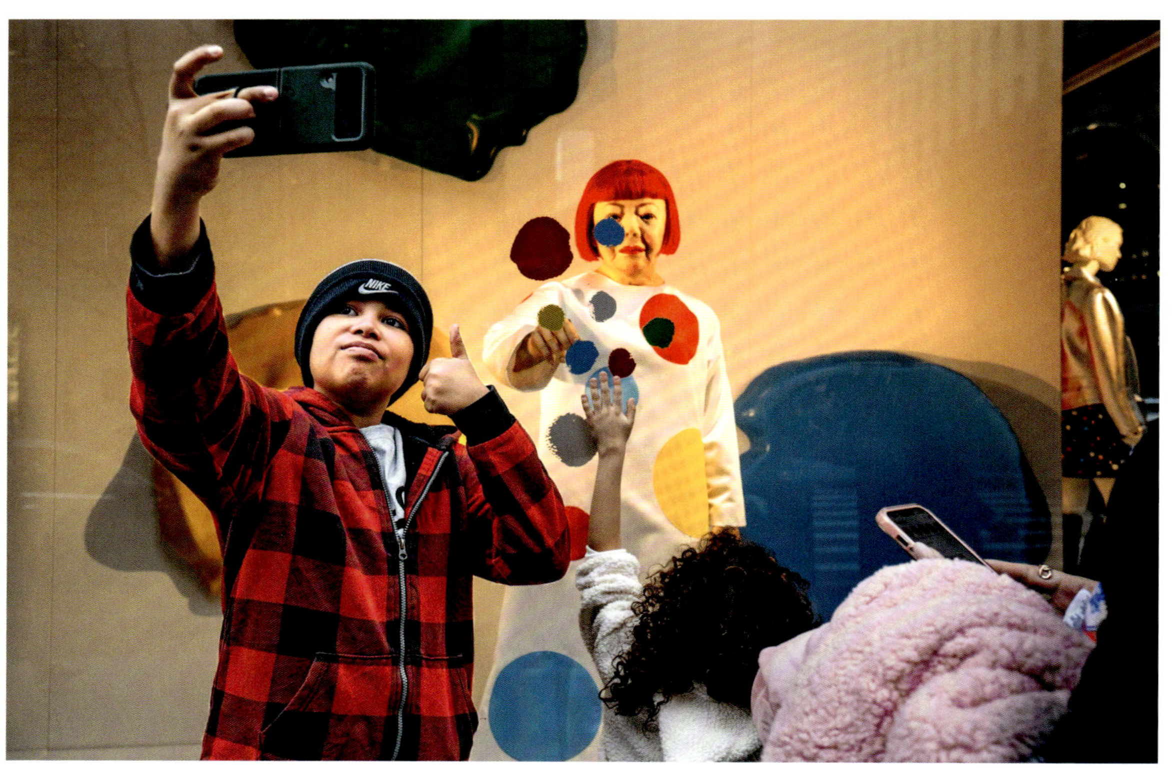

NIKE

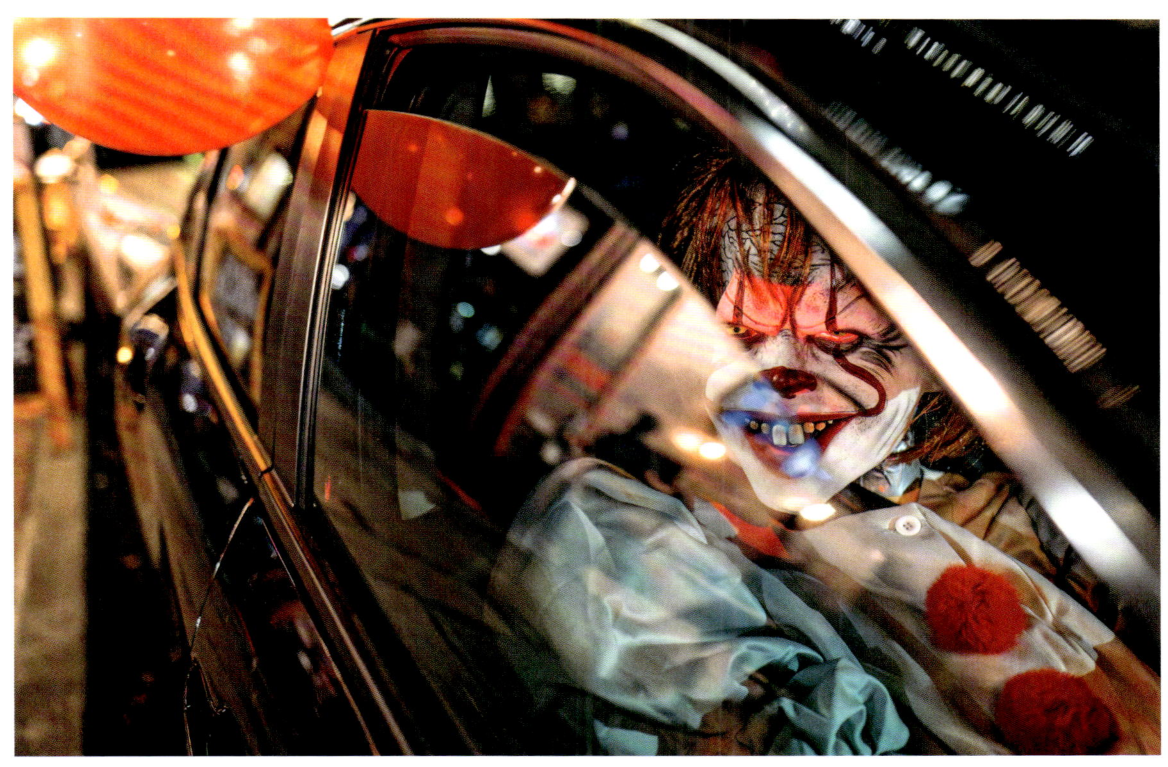

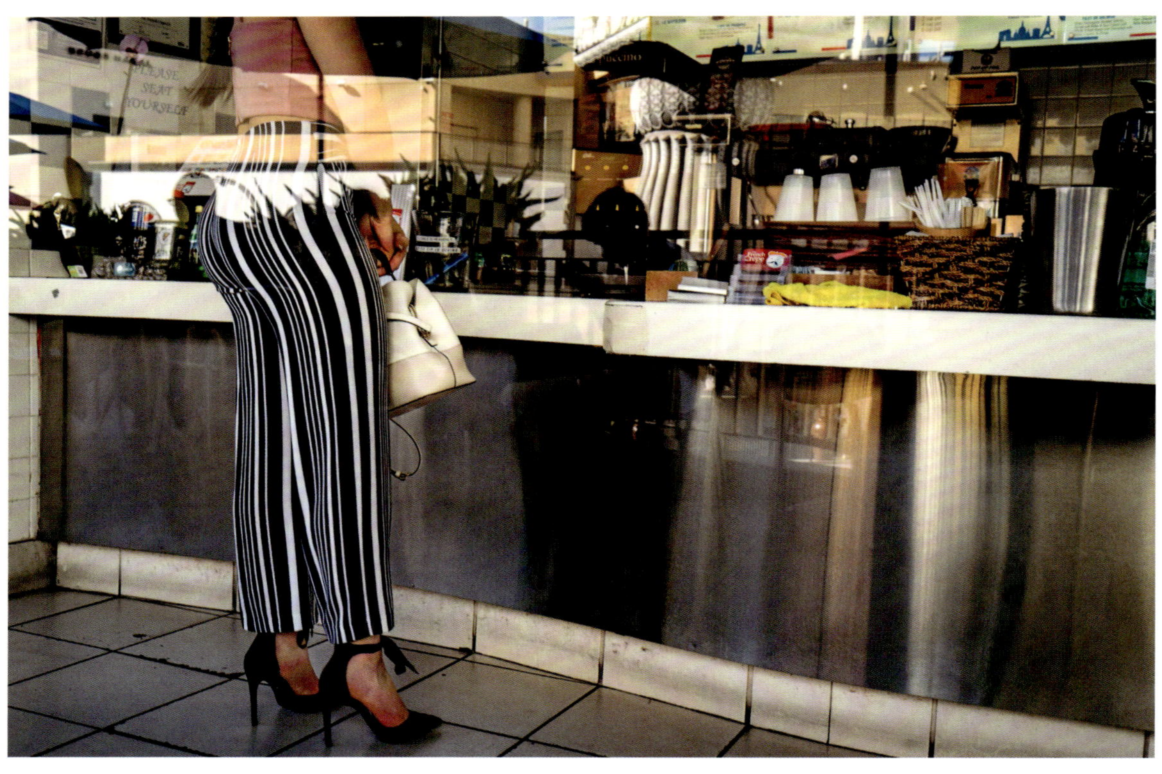
PLEASE
SEAT
YOURSELF

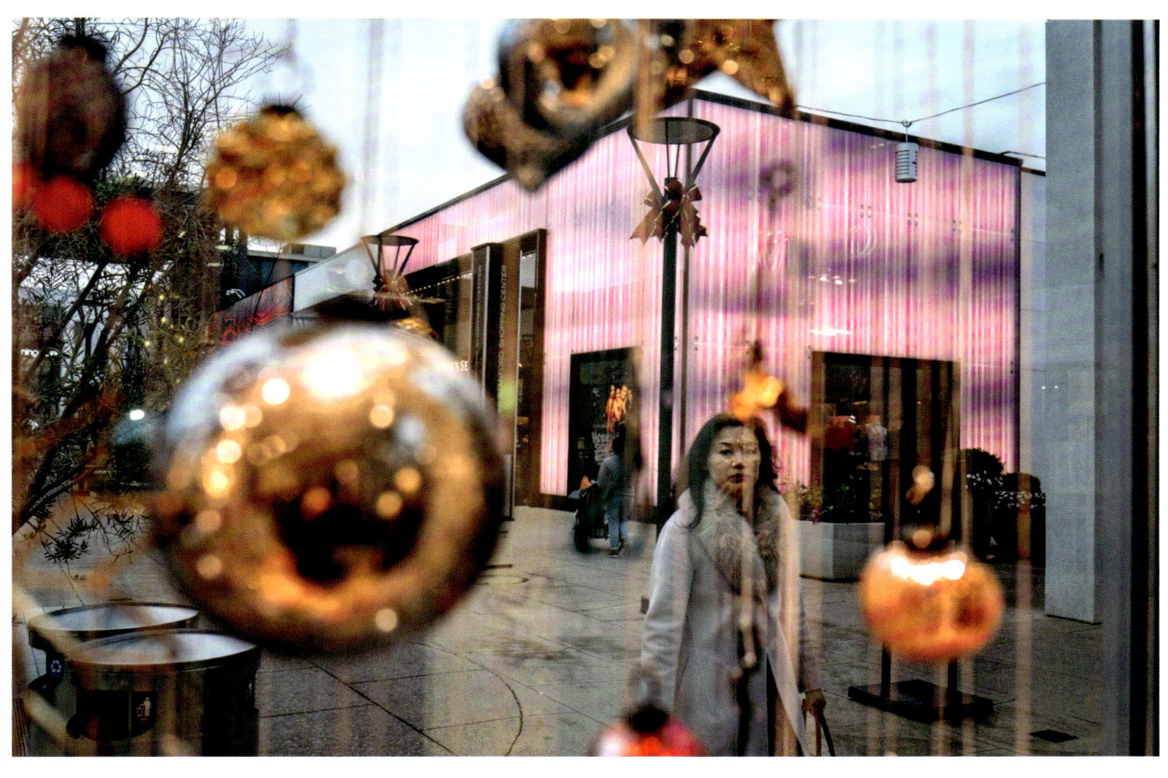

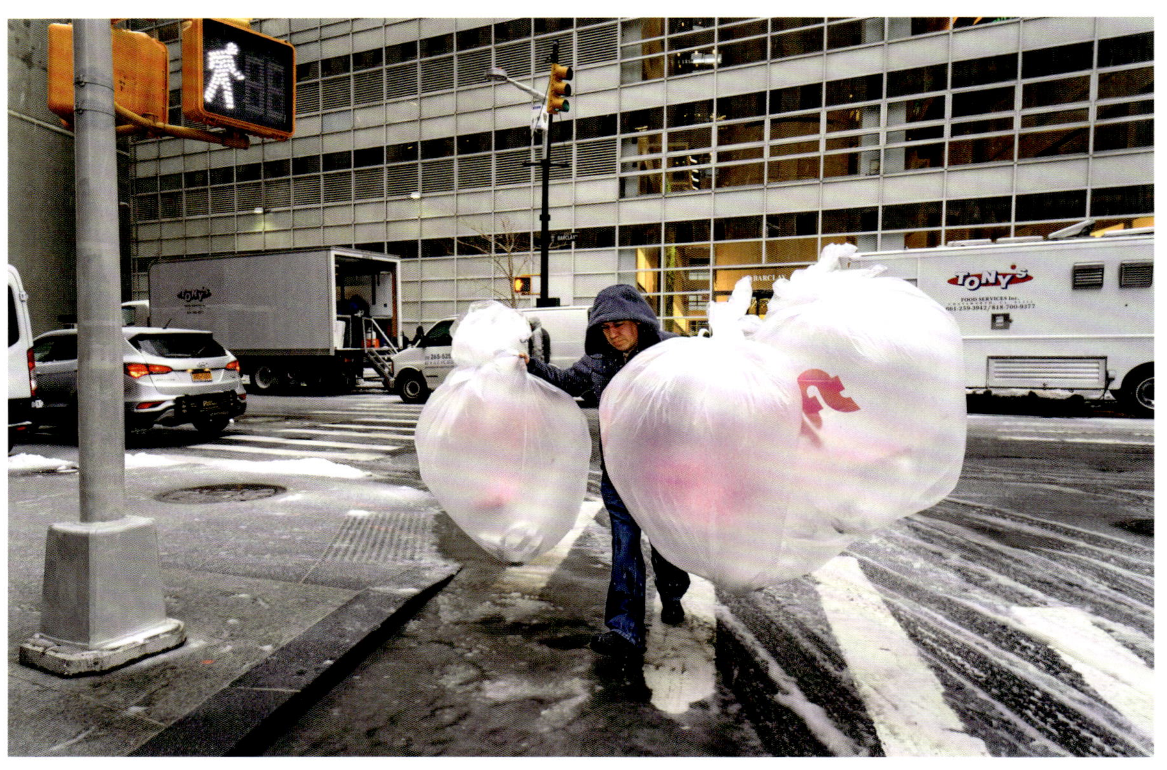

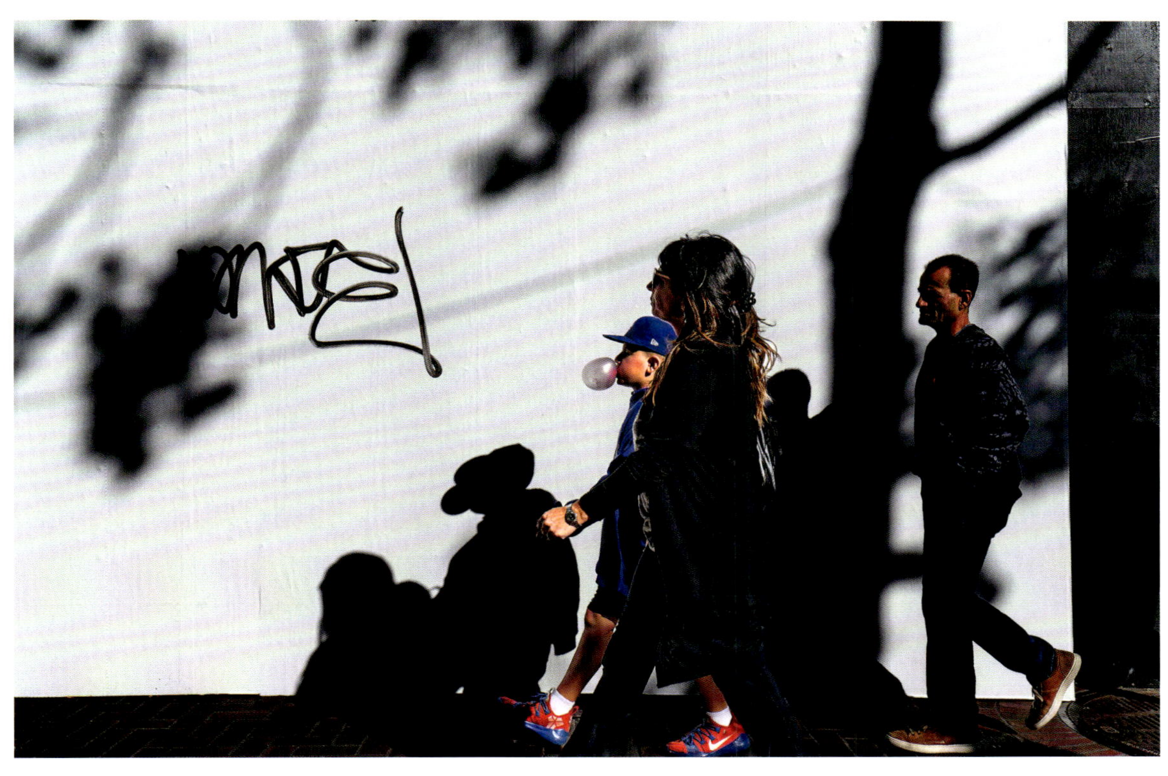

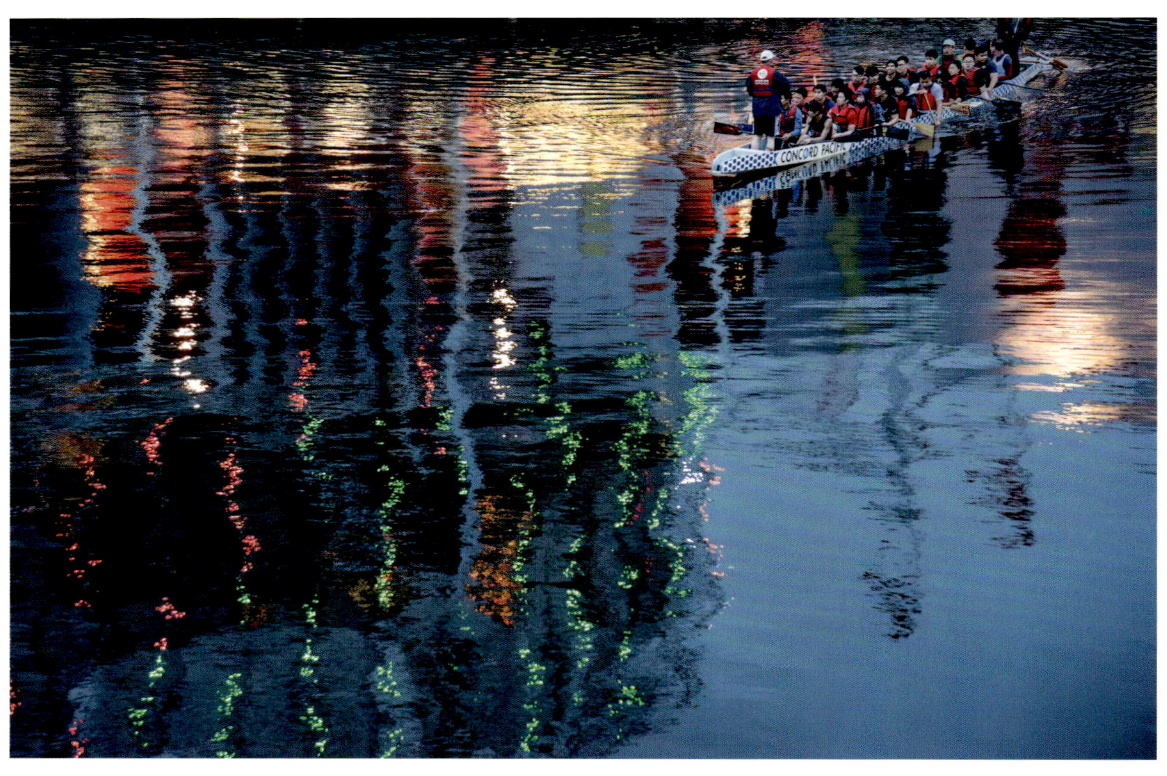

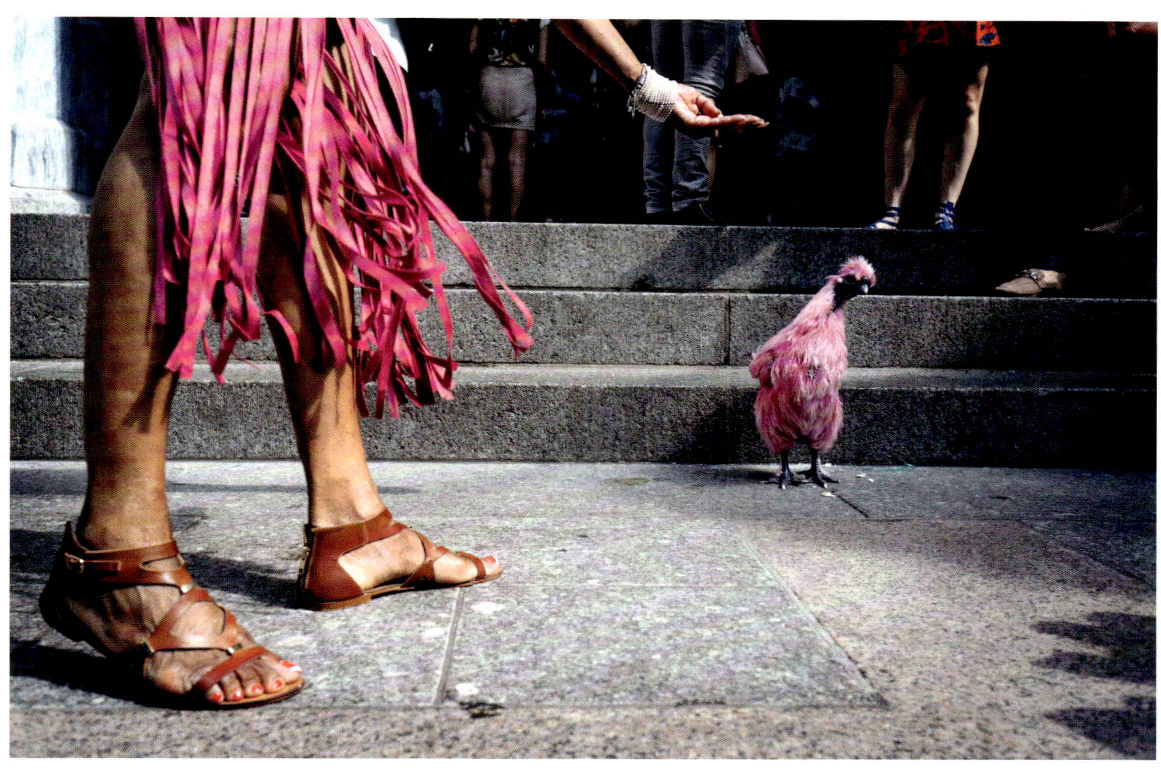

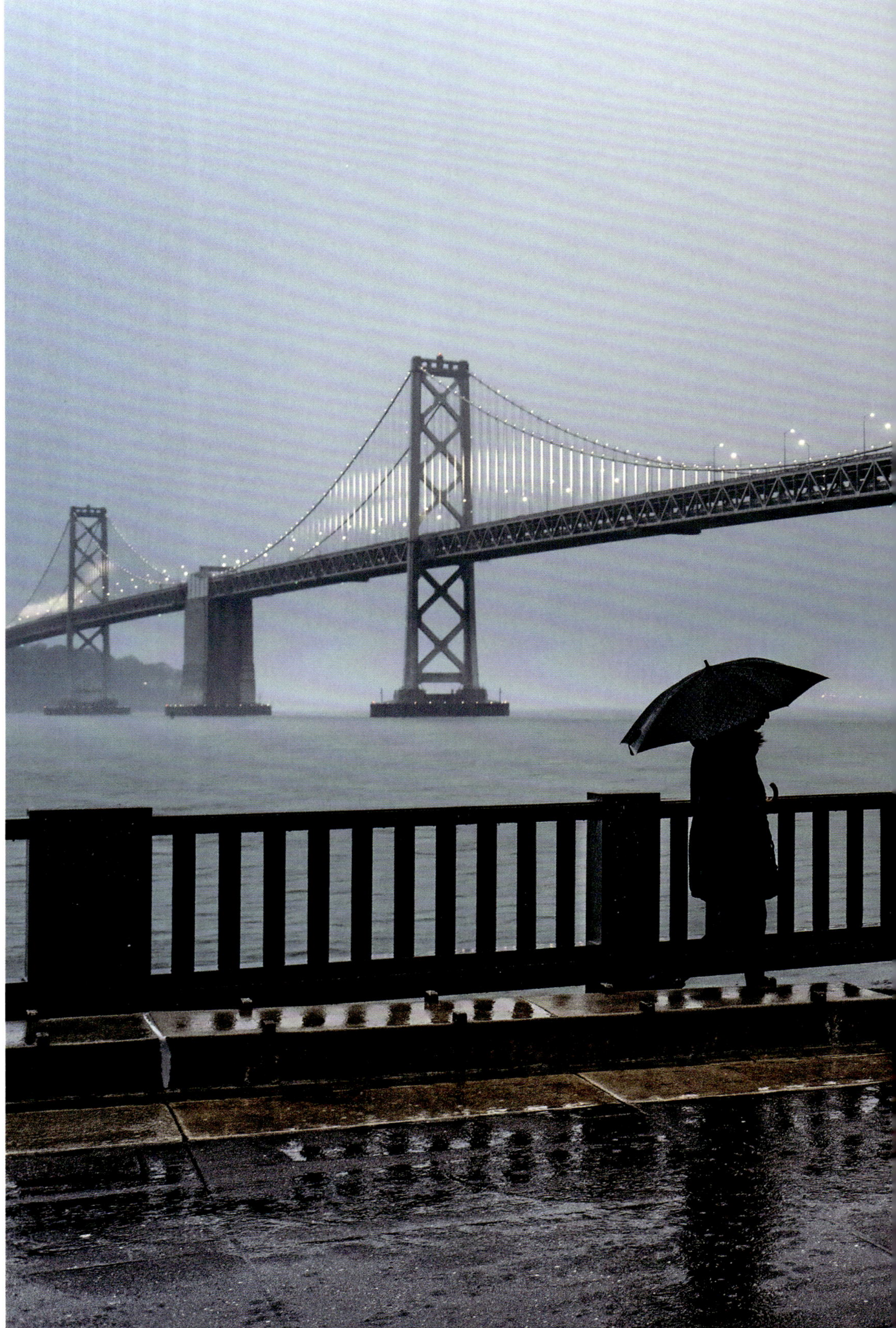

Don't put away your camera. Keep it out at all times even when you think you have the shot already.

—Mary Ellen Mark

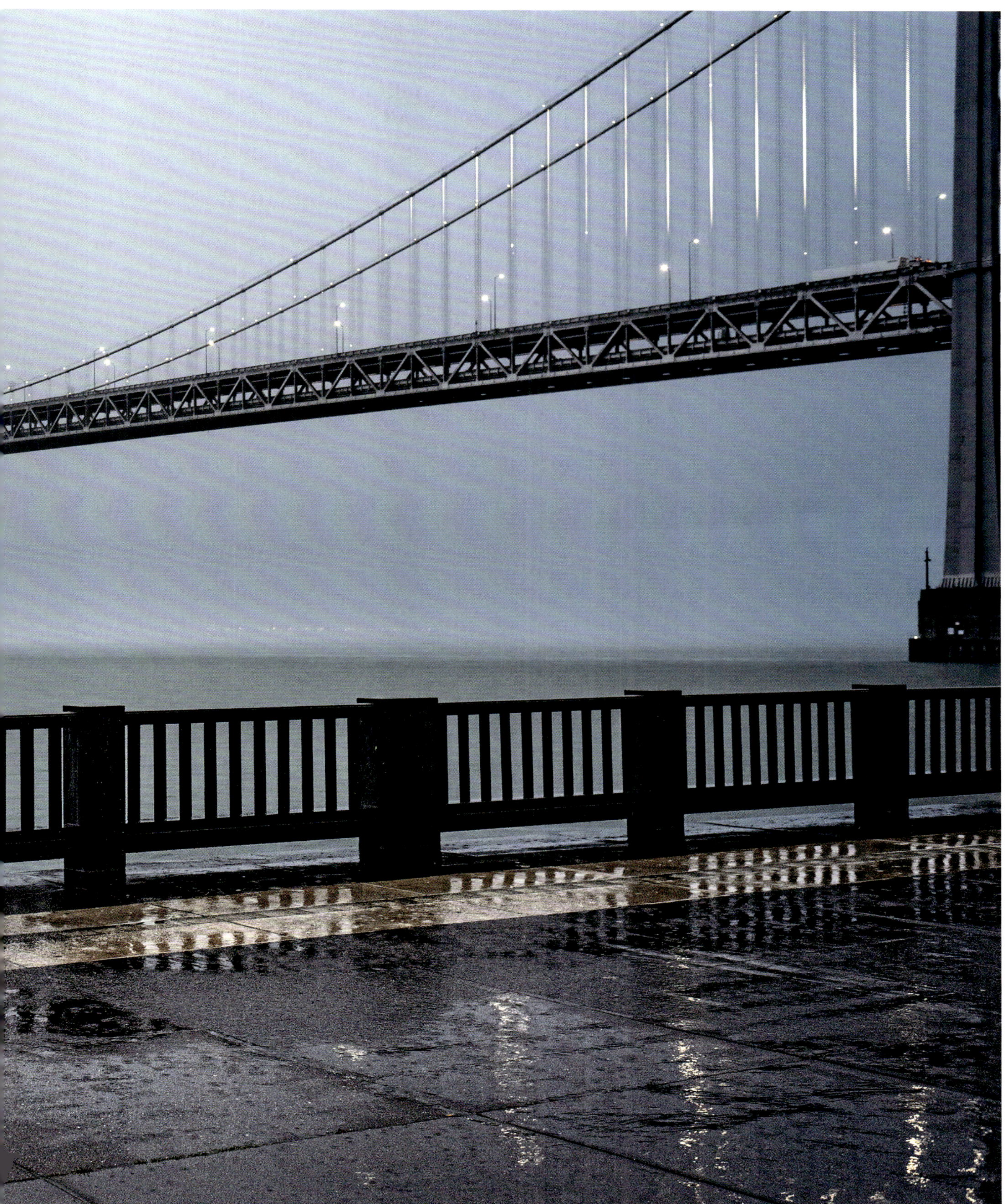

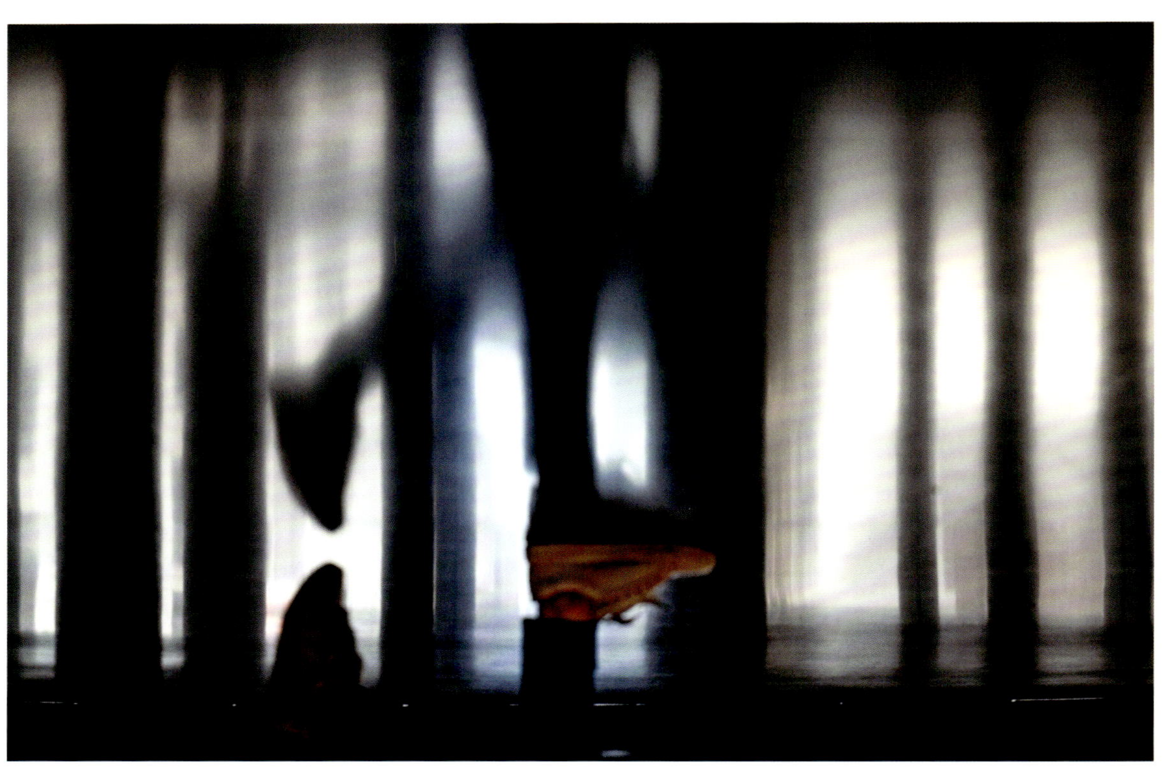

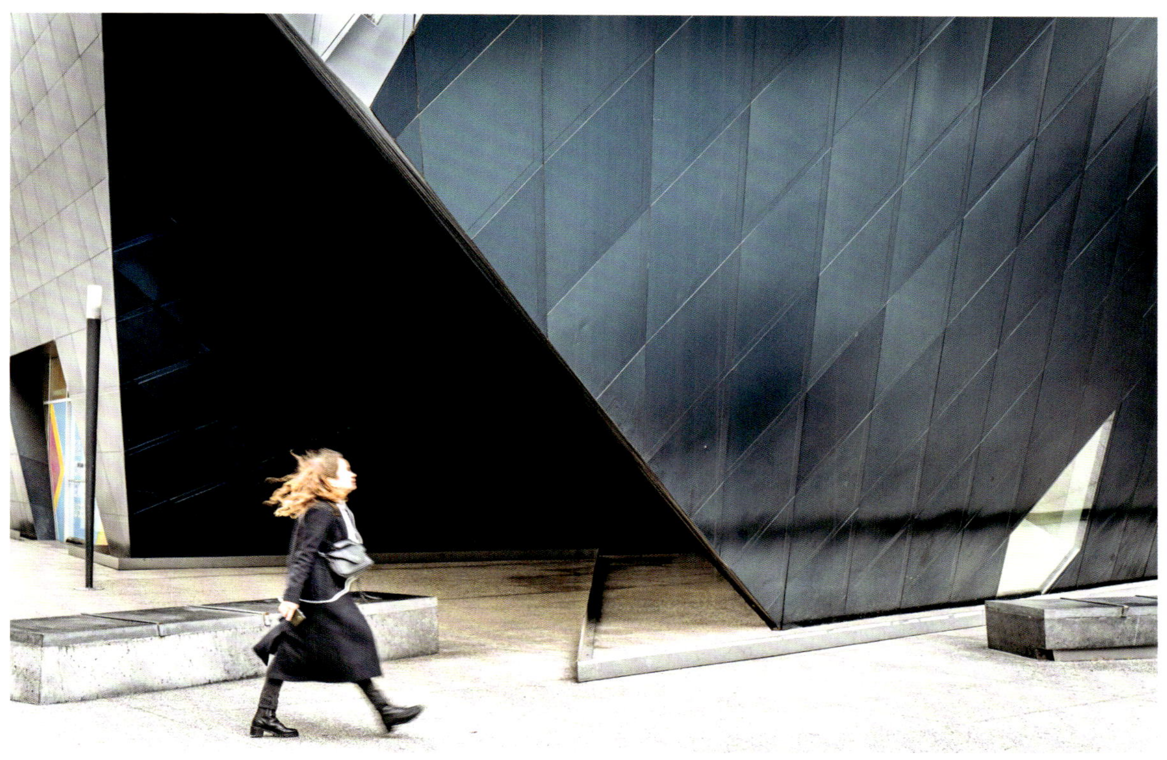

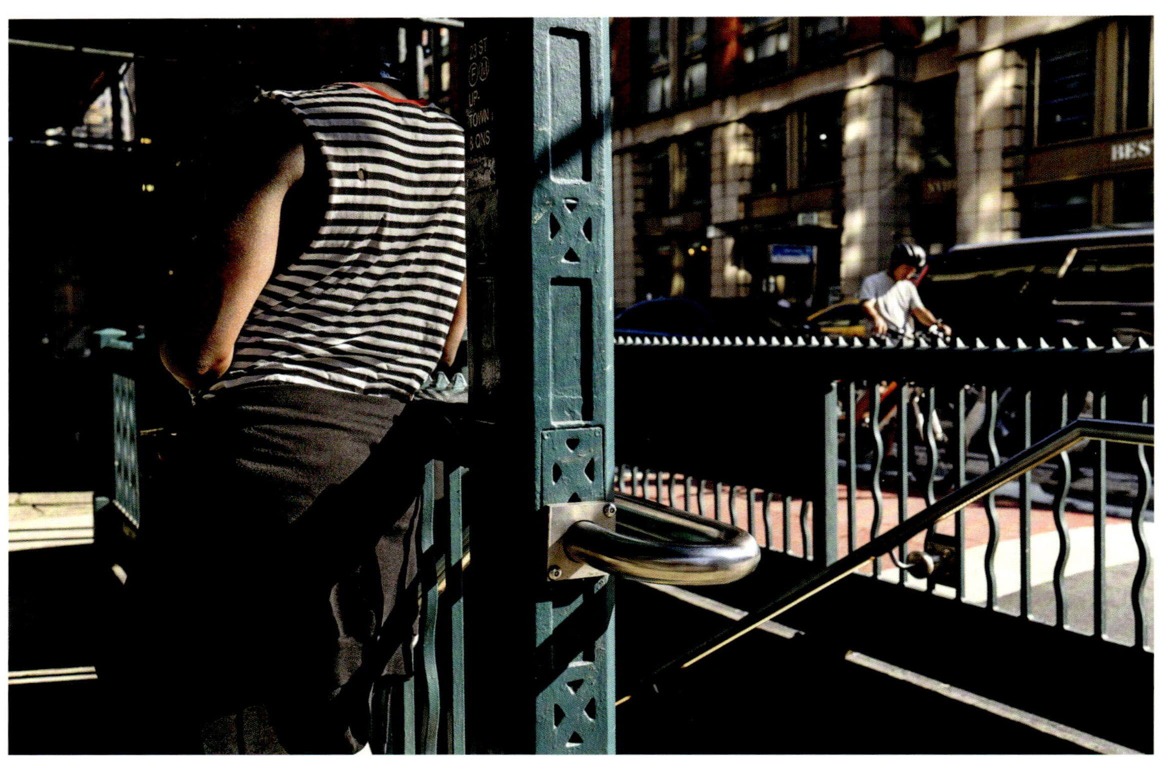

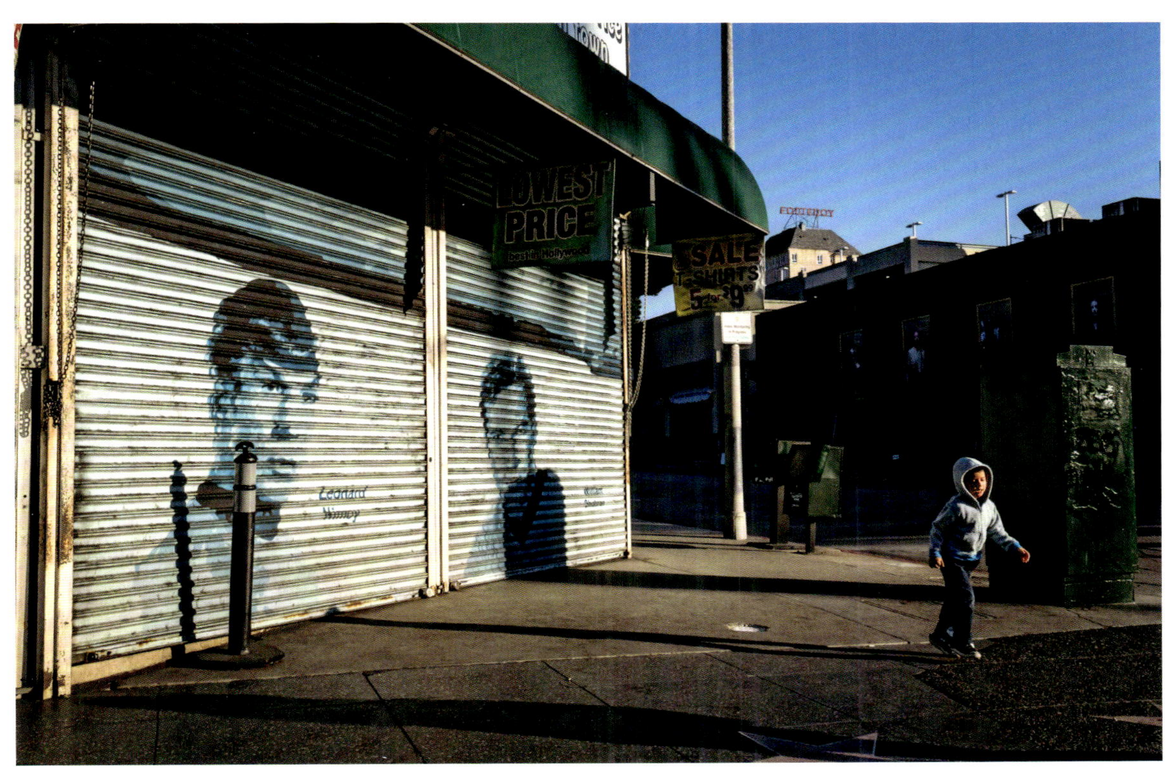

LOWEST
PRICE
SALE
T-SHIRTS
5 for $9.99

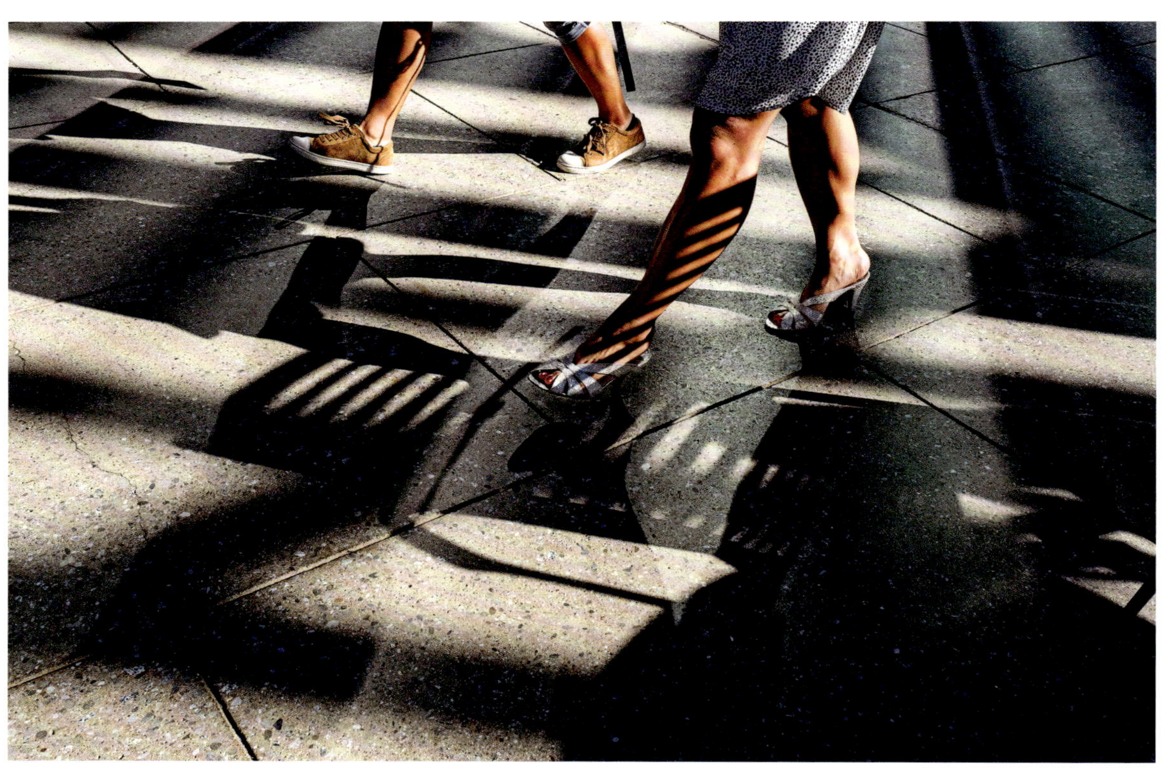

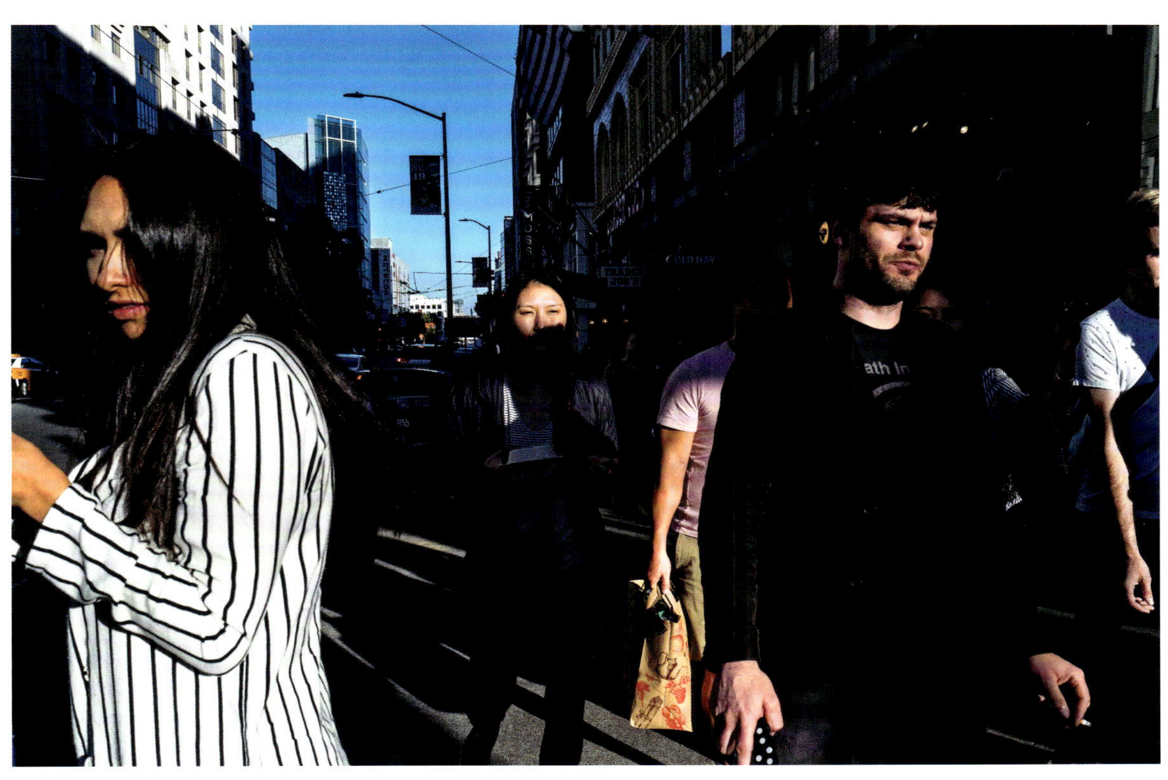

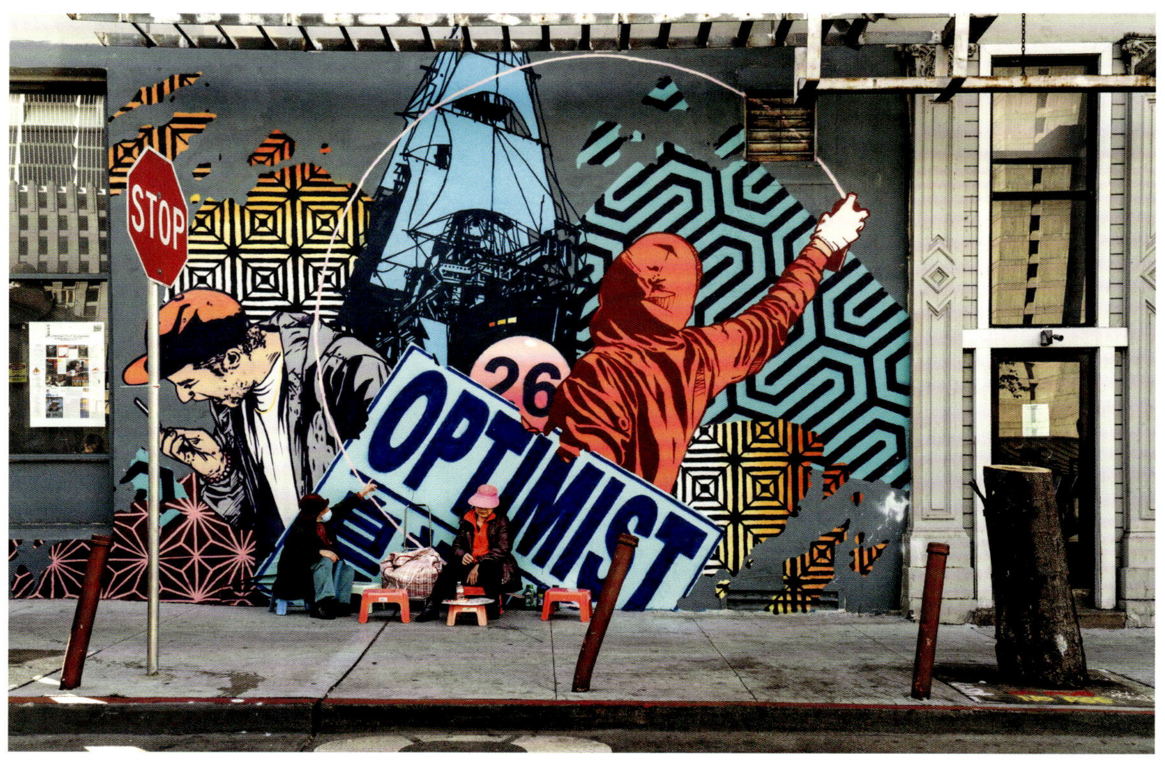
STOP
26
OPTIMIST

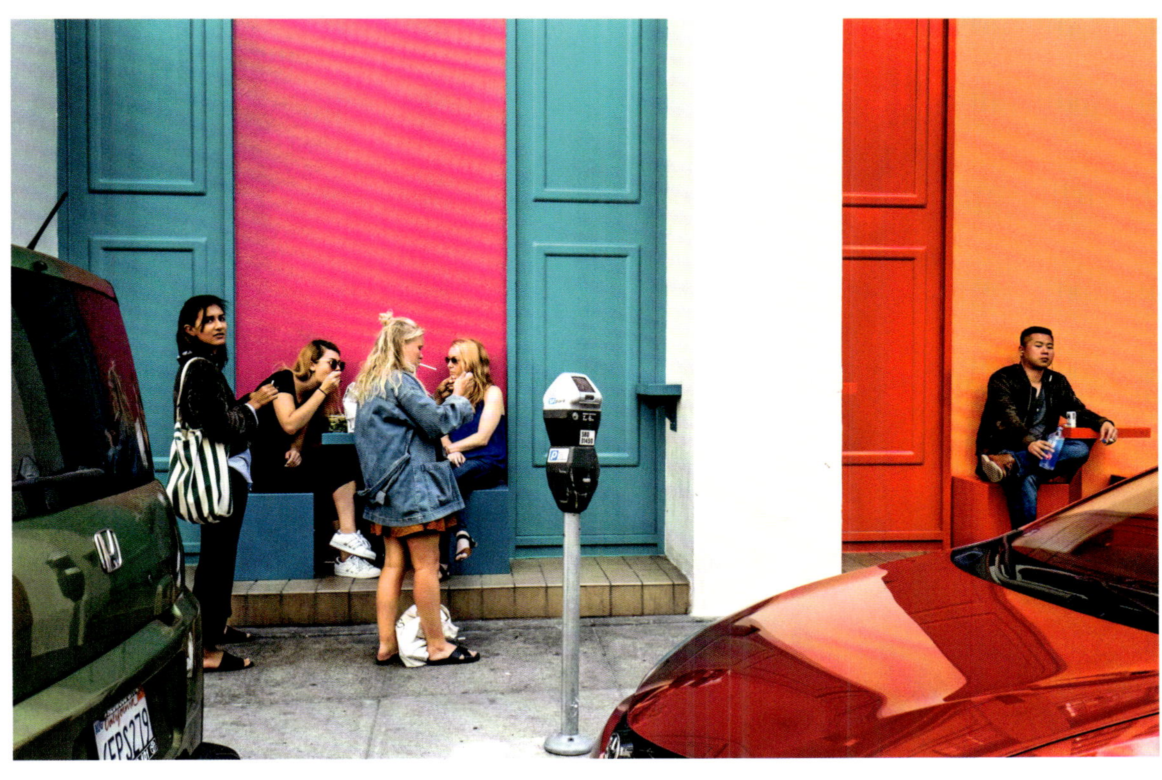

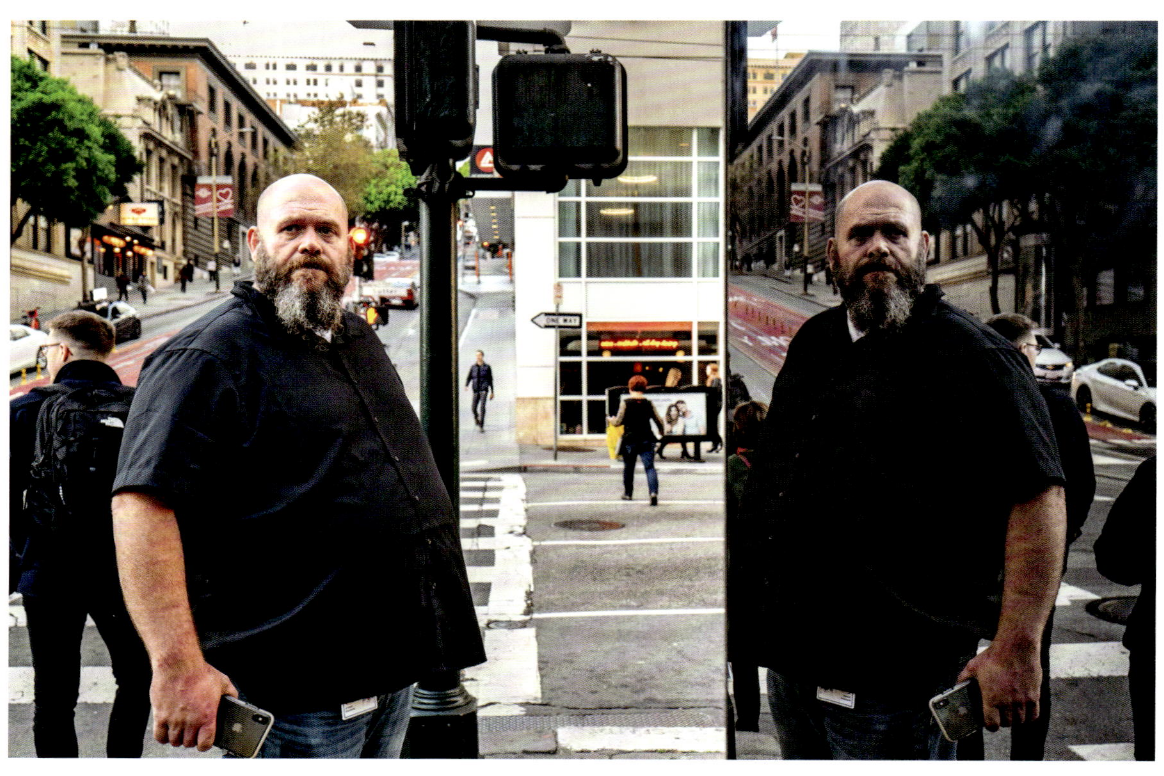

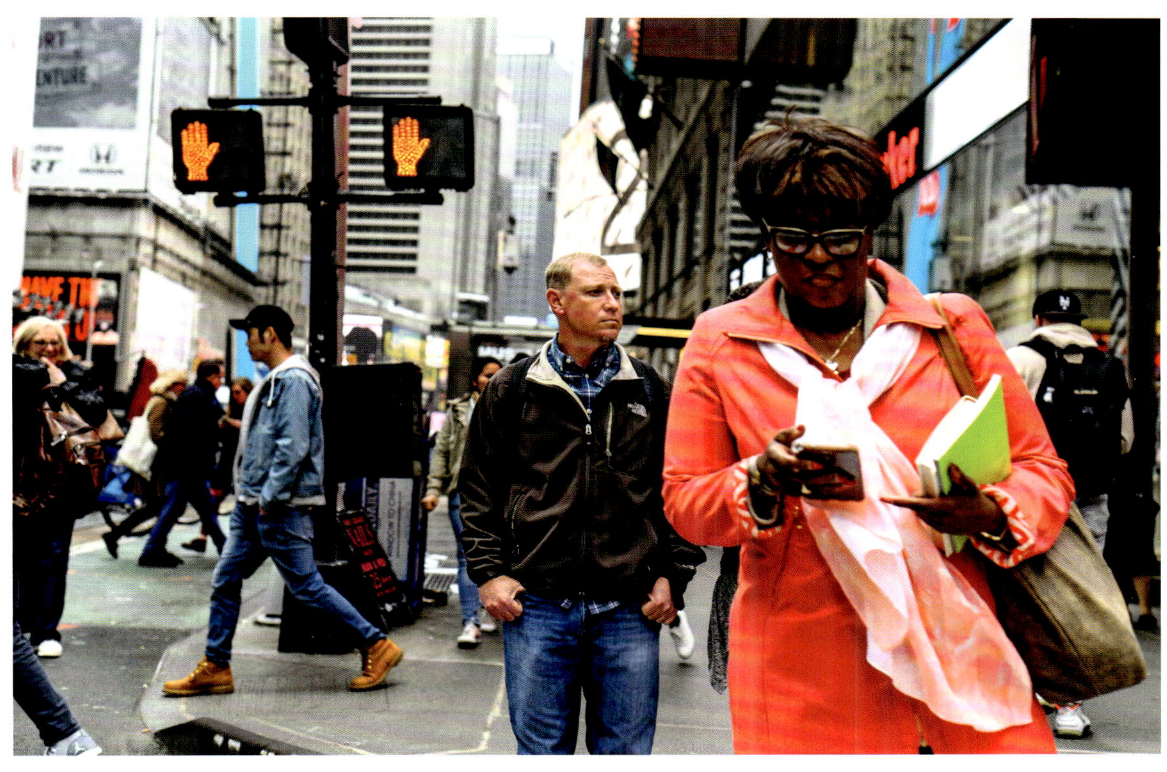

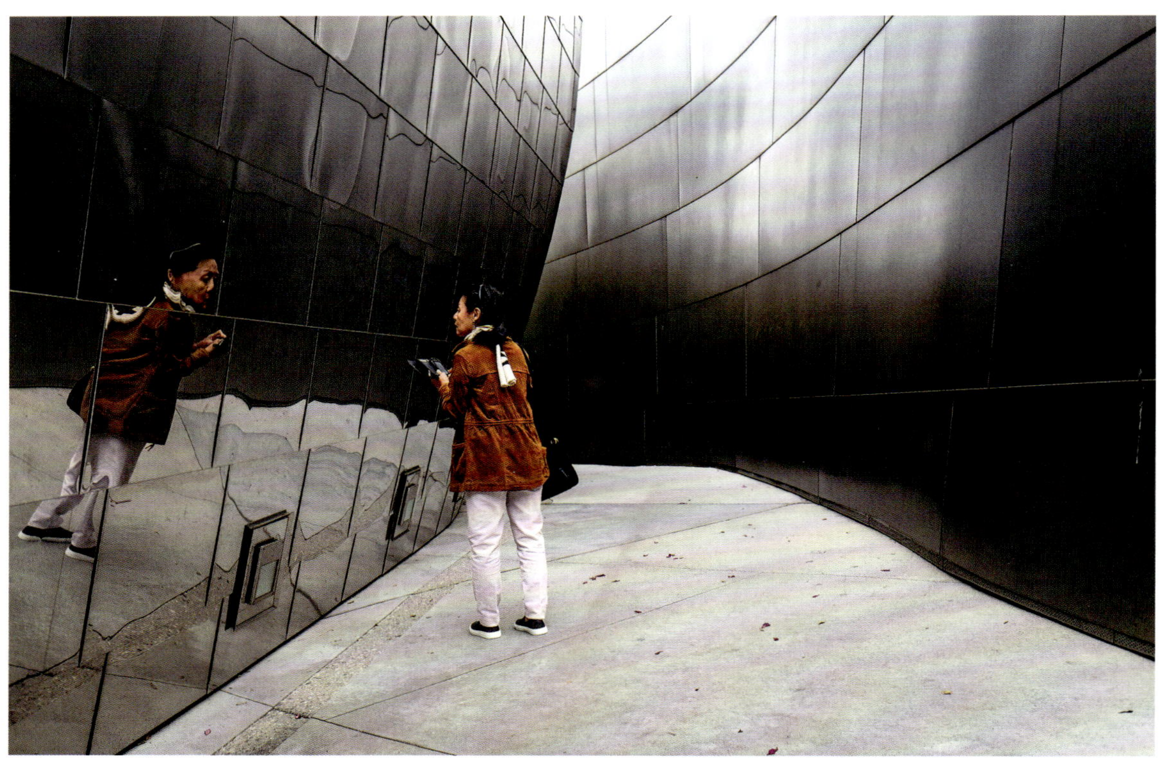

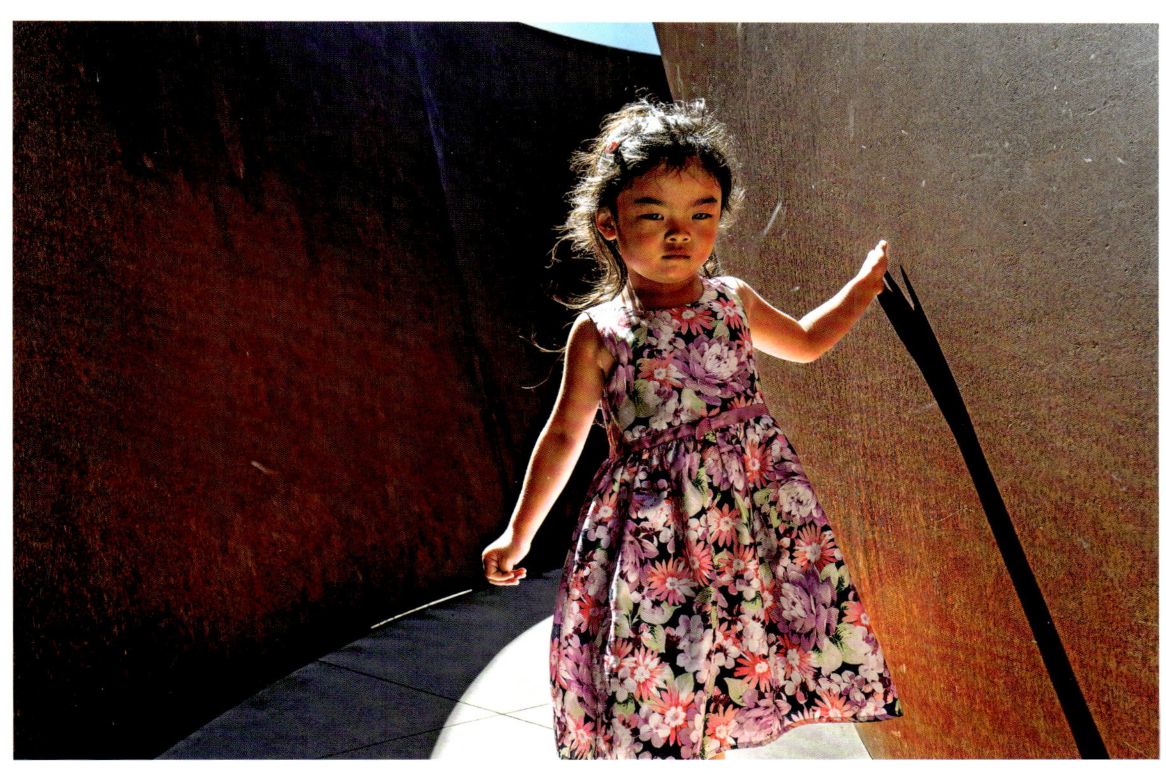

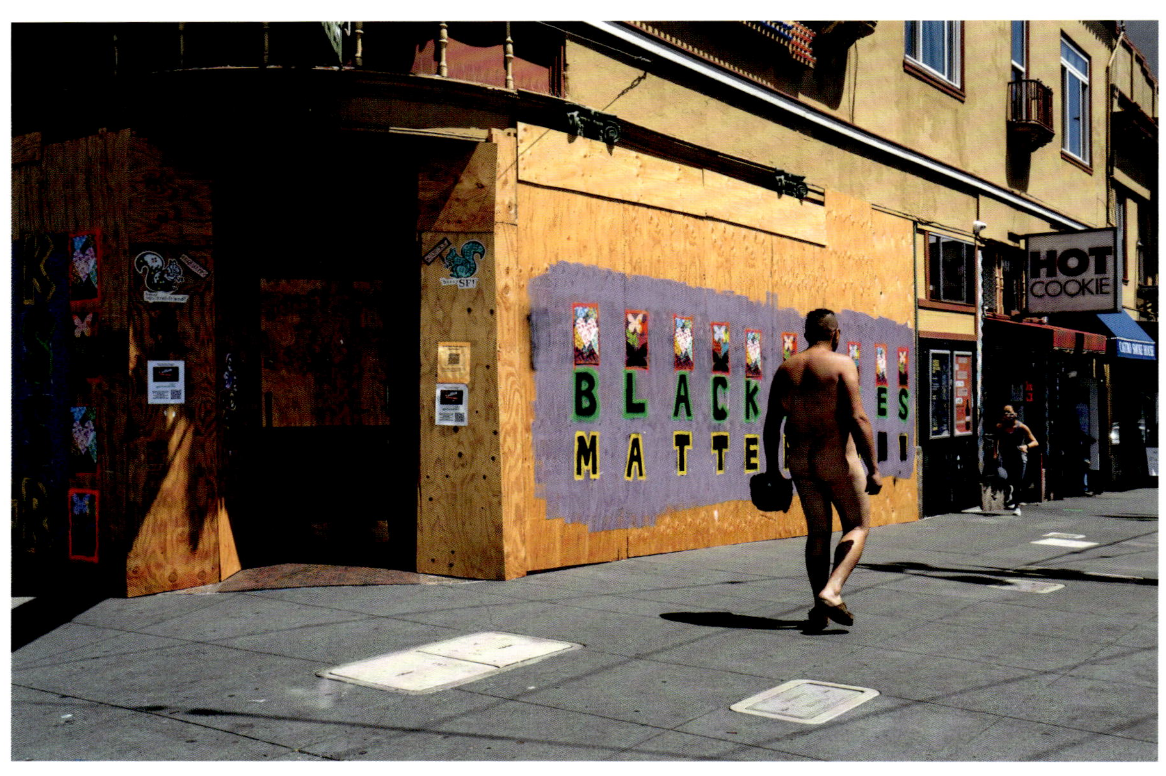
HOT
COOKIE
BLACK
MATTE

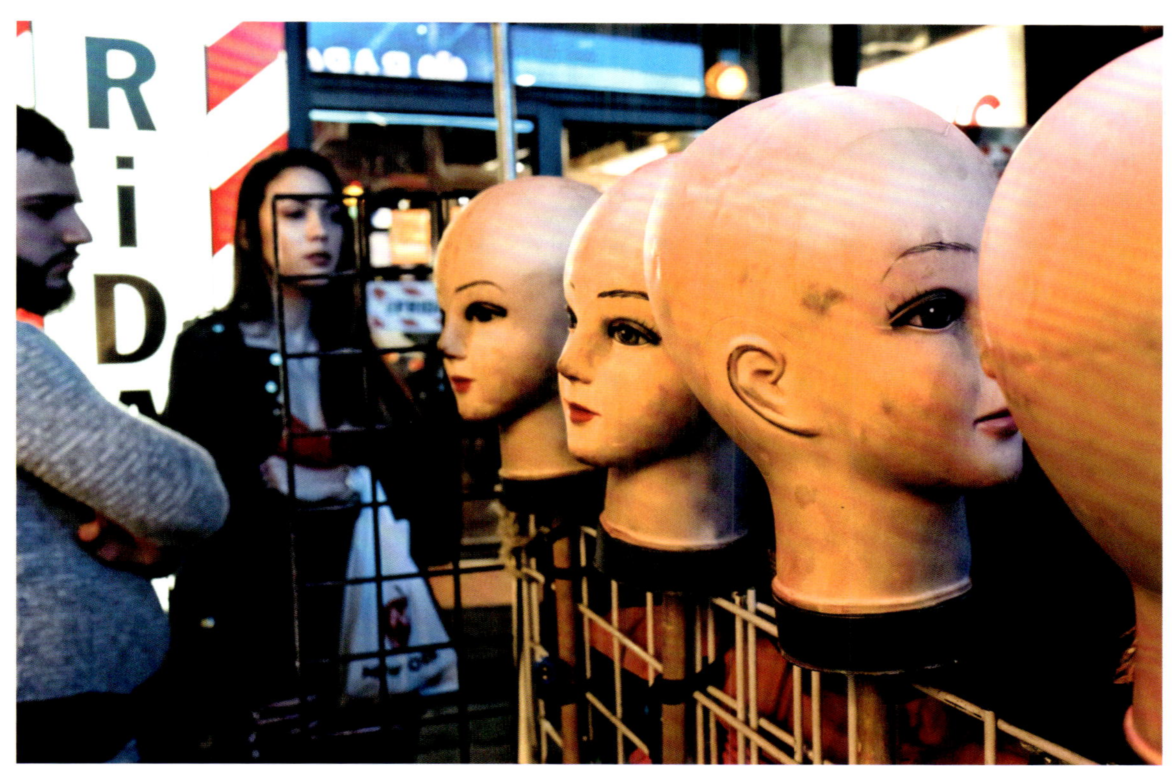

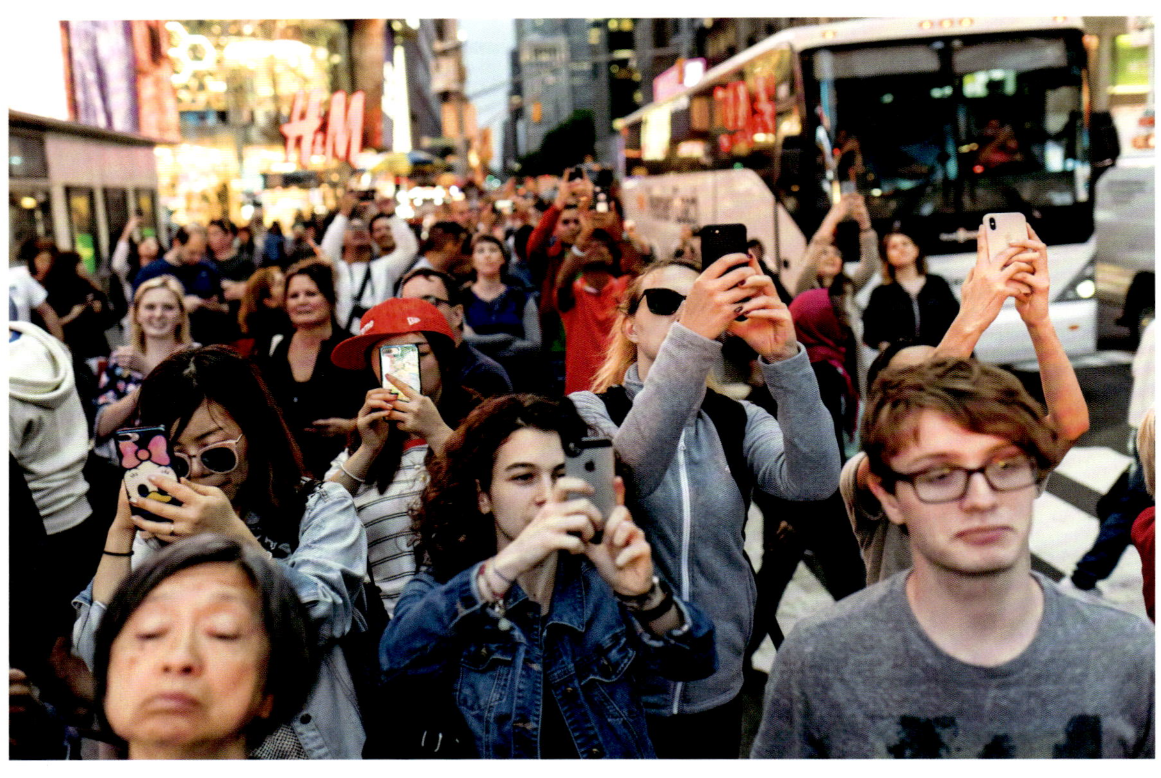

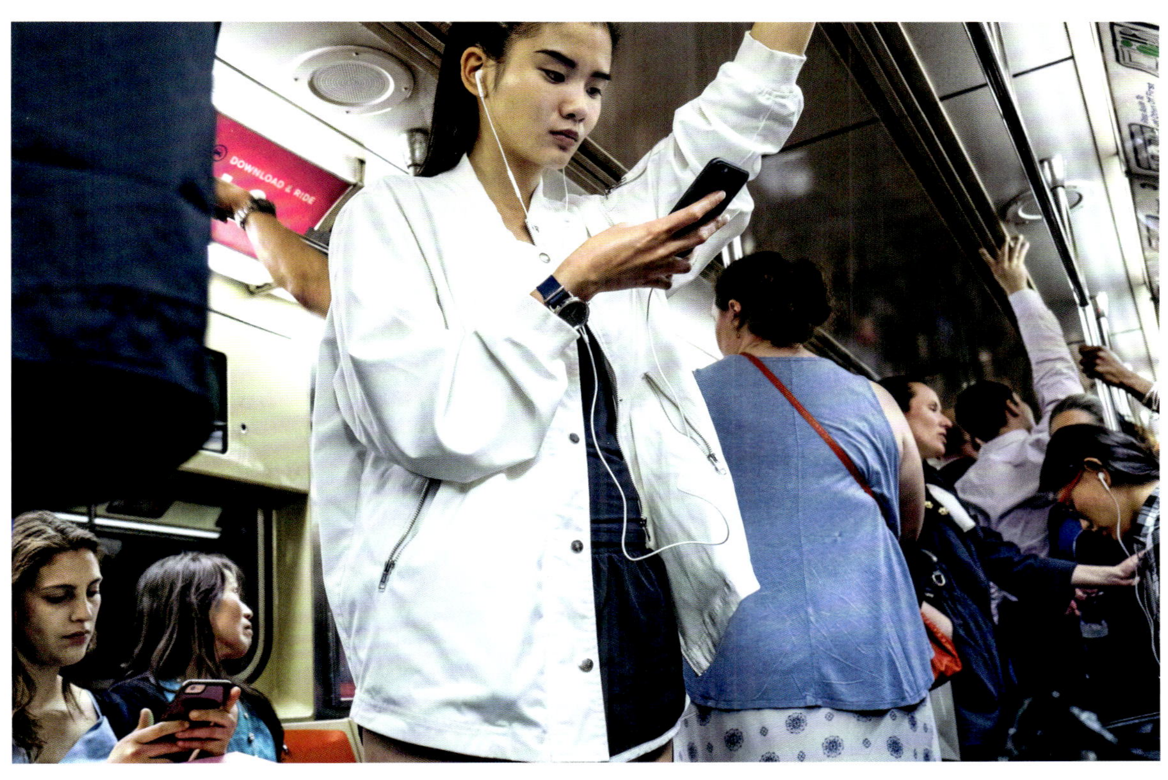

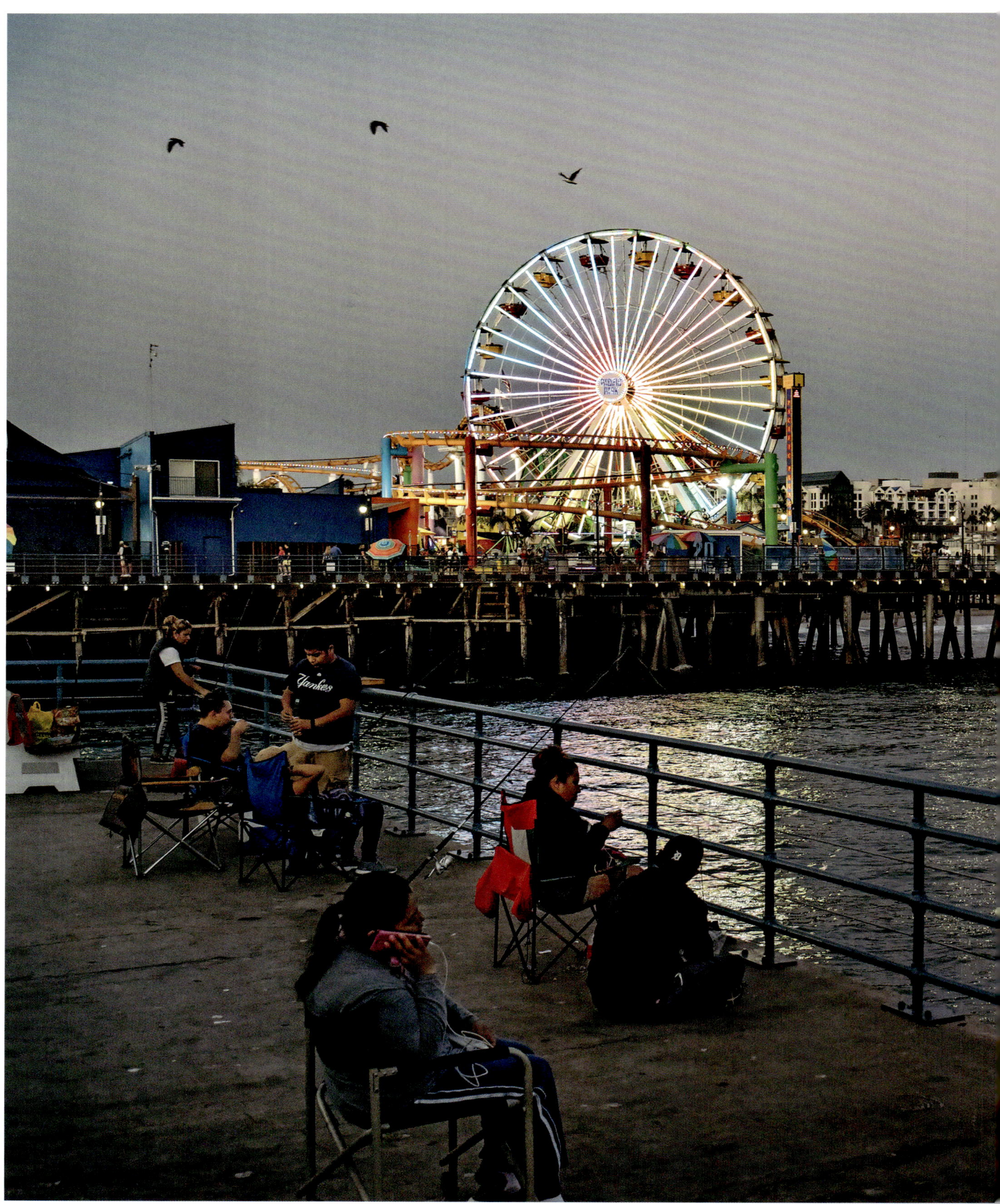

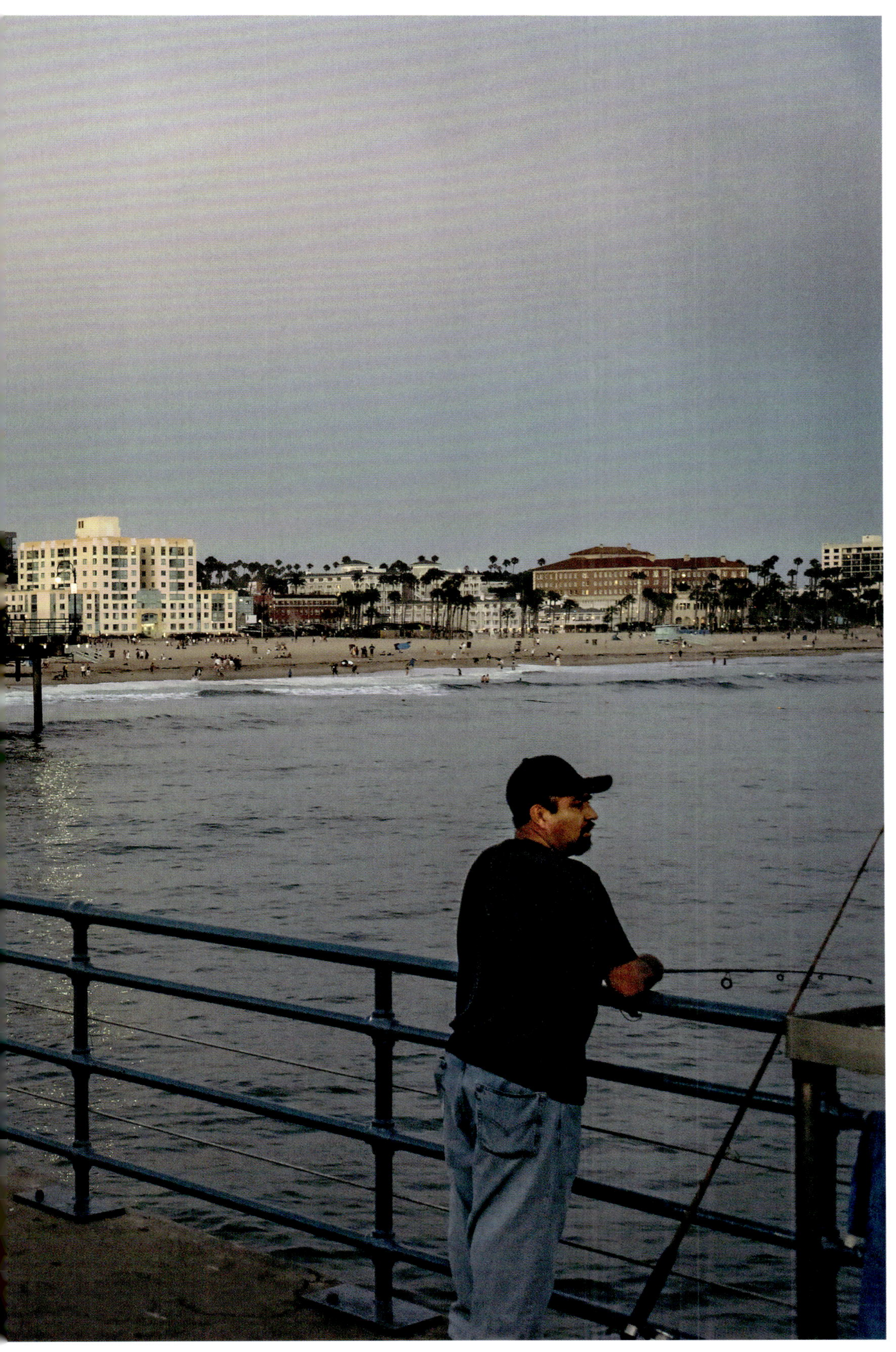

It's never easy
to work in the
city where you
live. I think my
photographs say
something about
the current moment
and the places in
which they were
taken. I always hope
to transmit a certain
joy for life through
my images.

—Harry Gruyaert

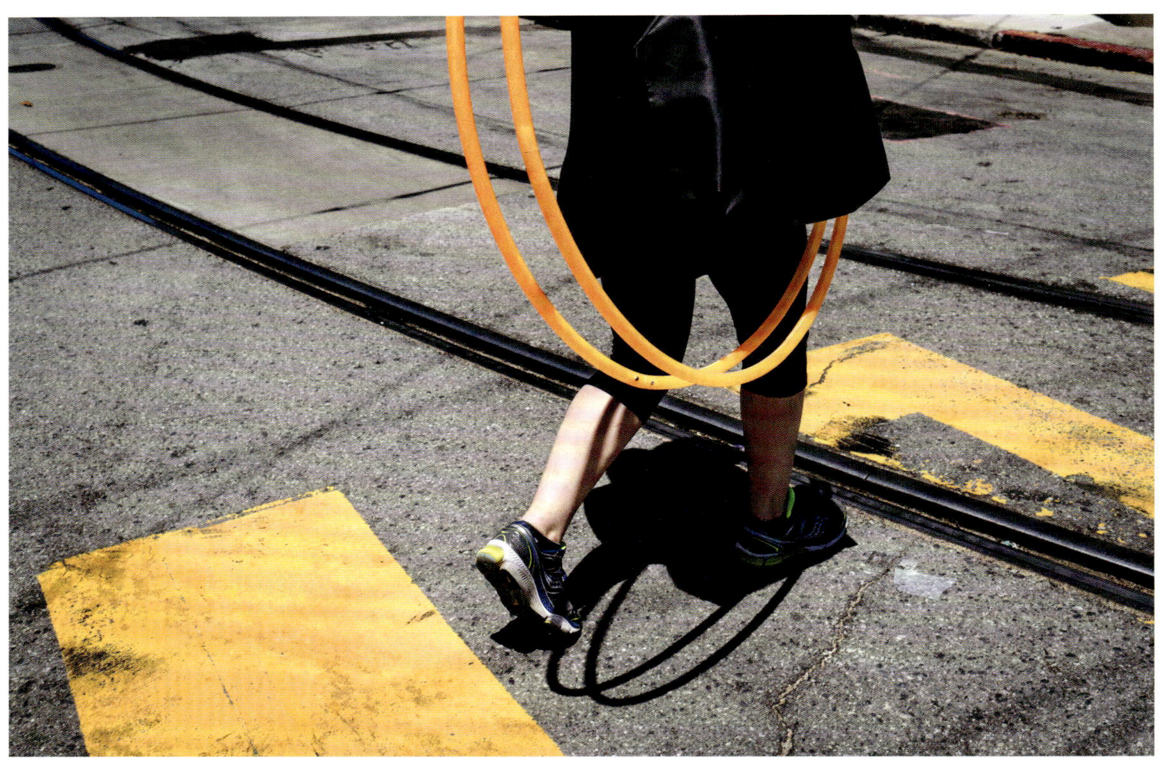

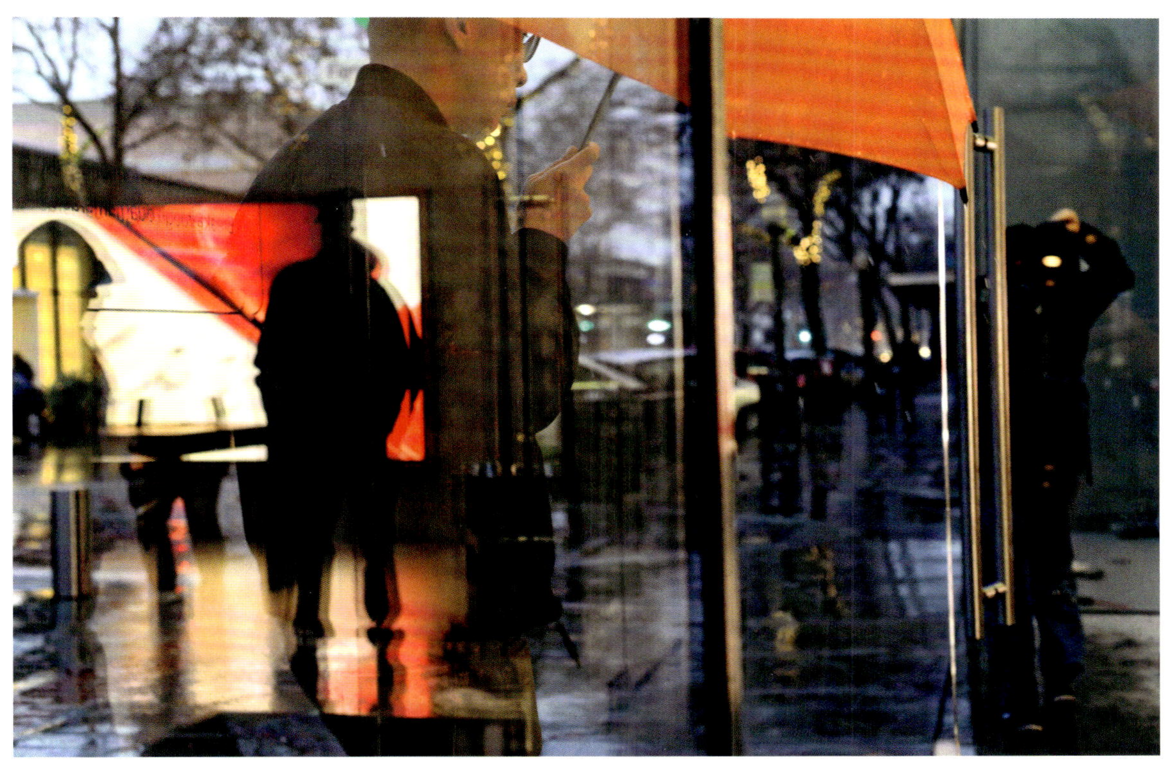

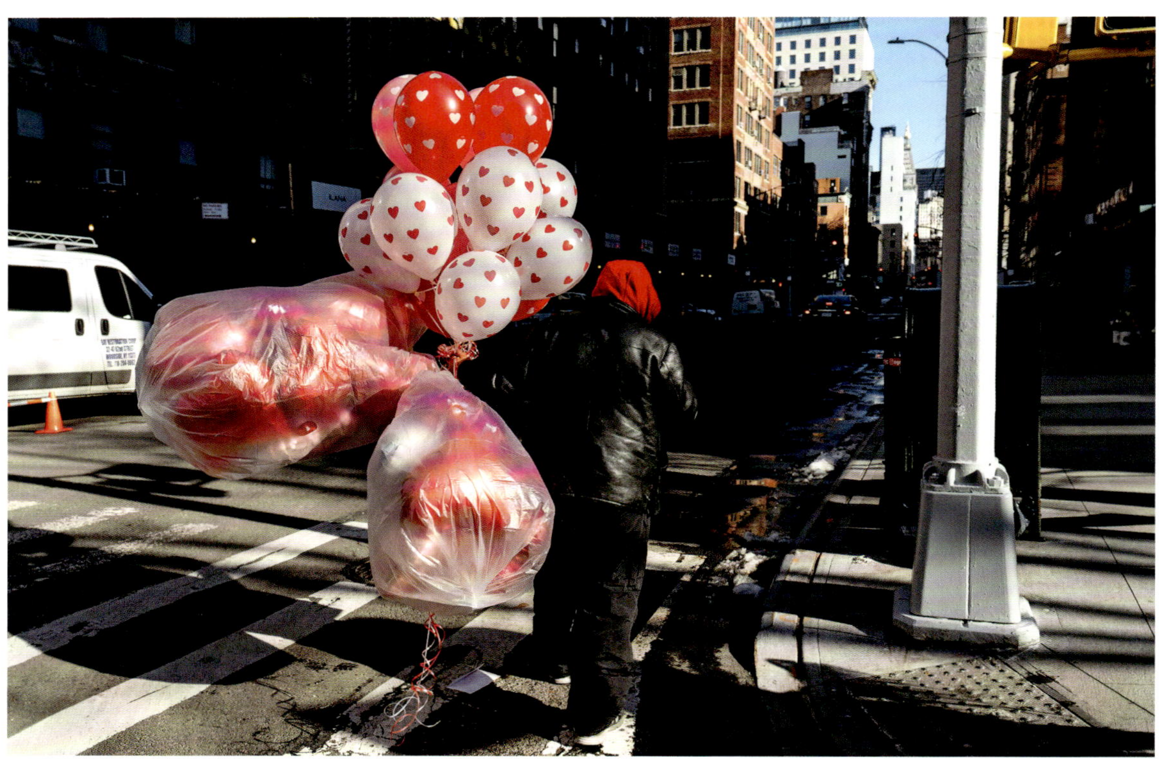

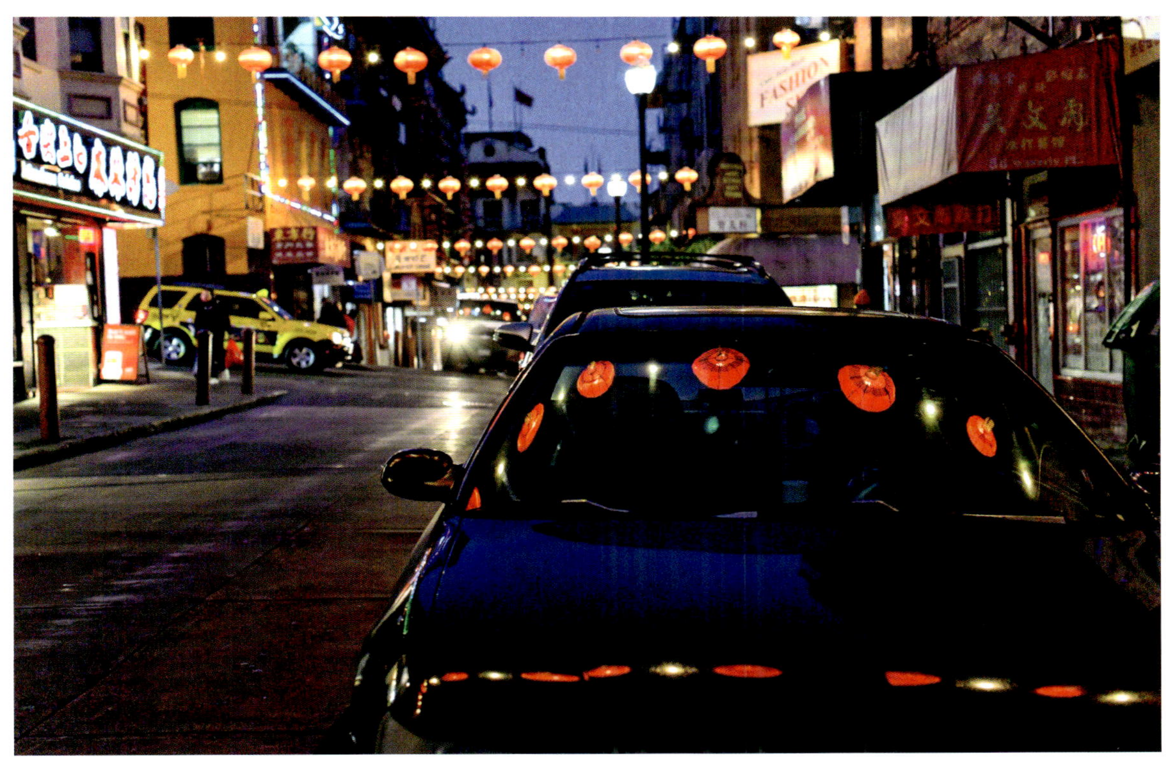

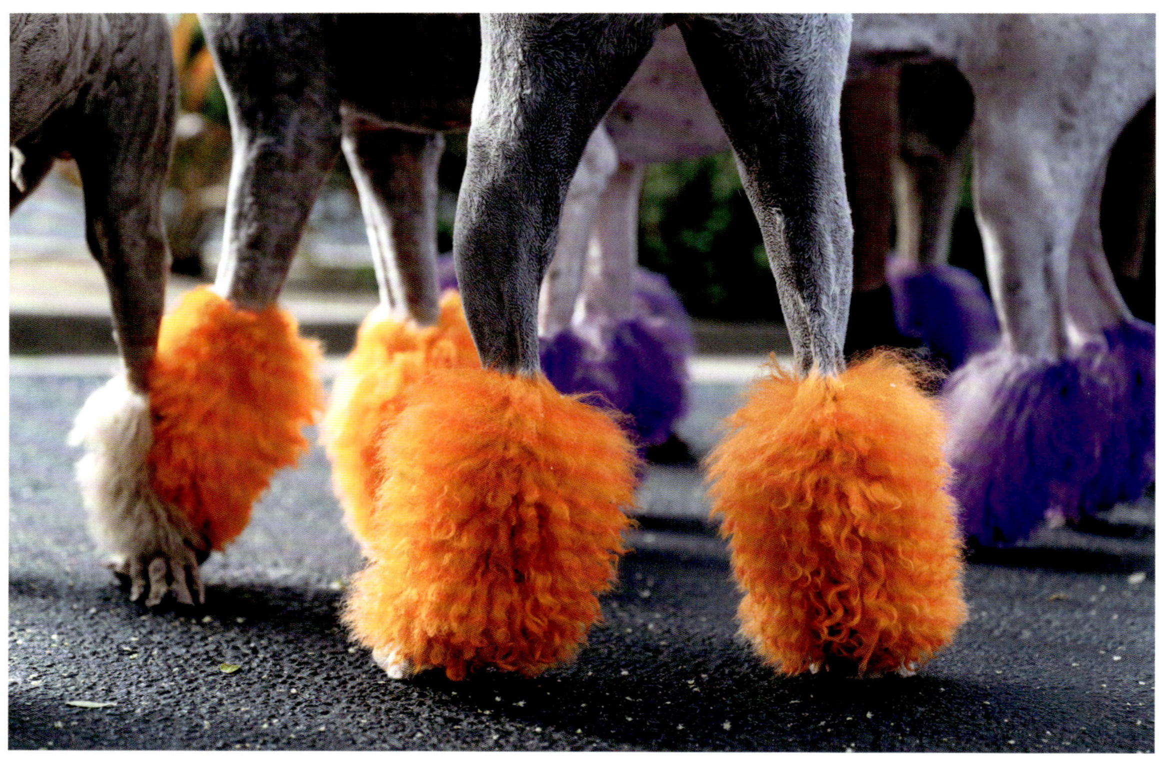

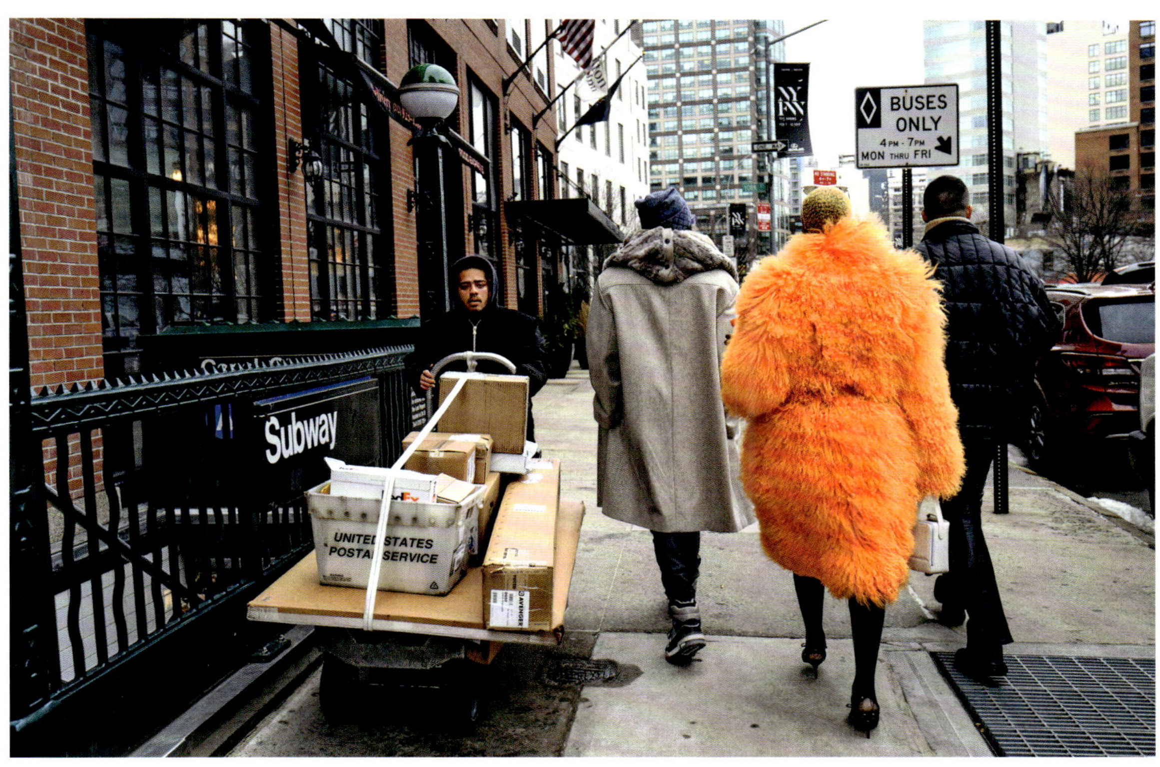
Subway
UNITED STATES
POSTAL SERVICE
BUSES
ONLY
4 PM - 7PM
MON THRU FRI

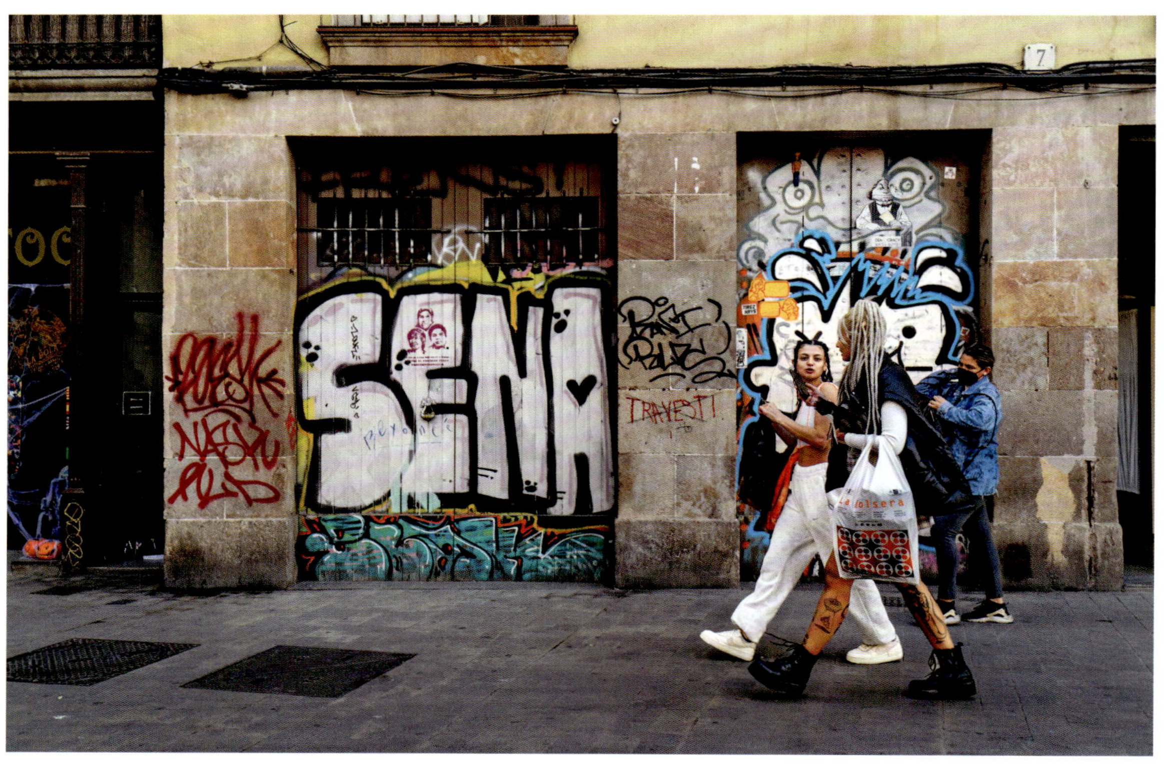

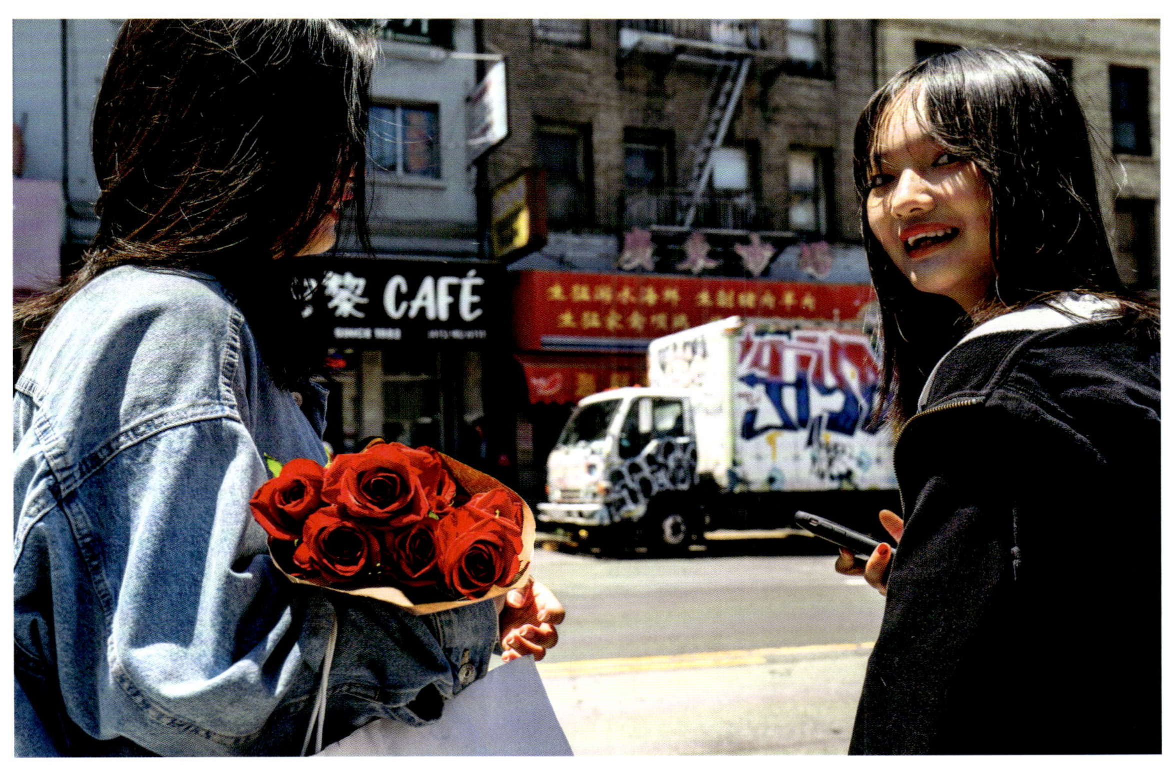
黎 CAFÉ

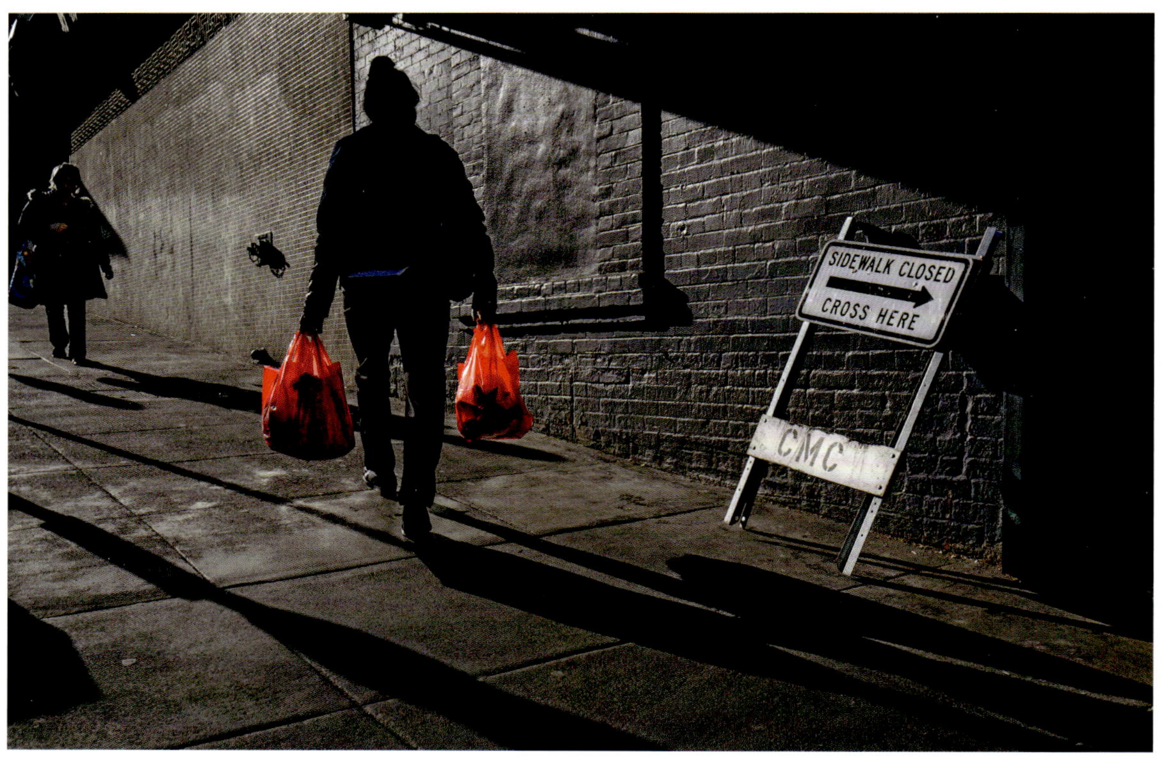

SIDEWALK CLOSED
CROSS HERE
CMC

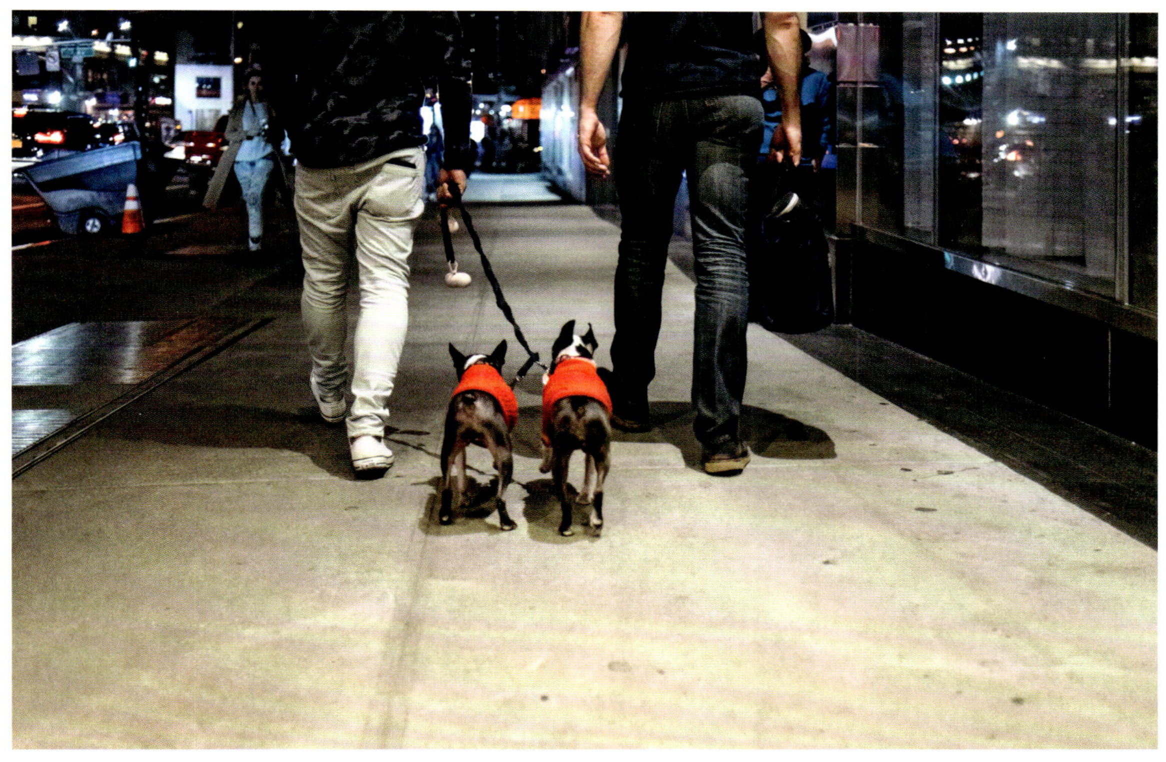

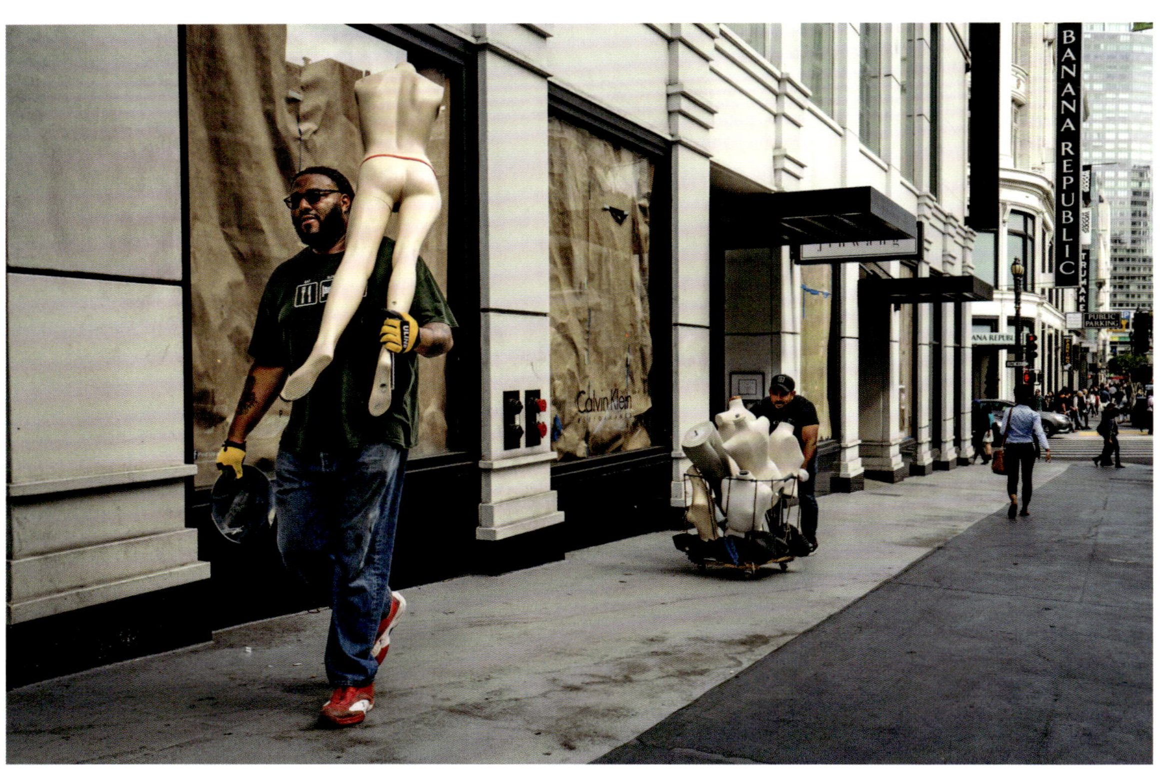

BANANA REPUBLIC
PUBLIC PARKING
Calvin Klein

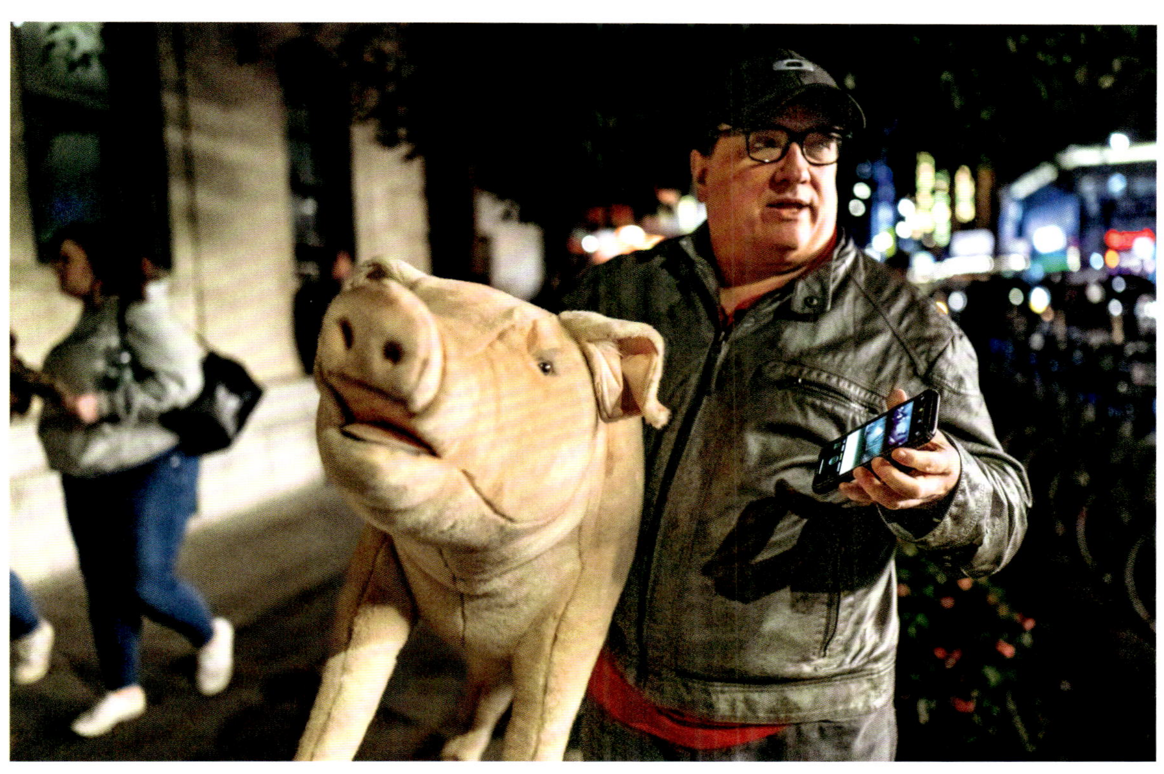

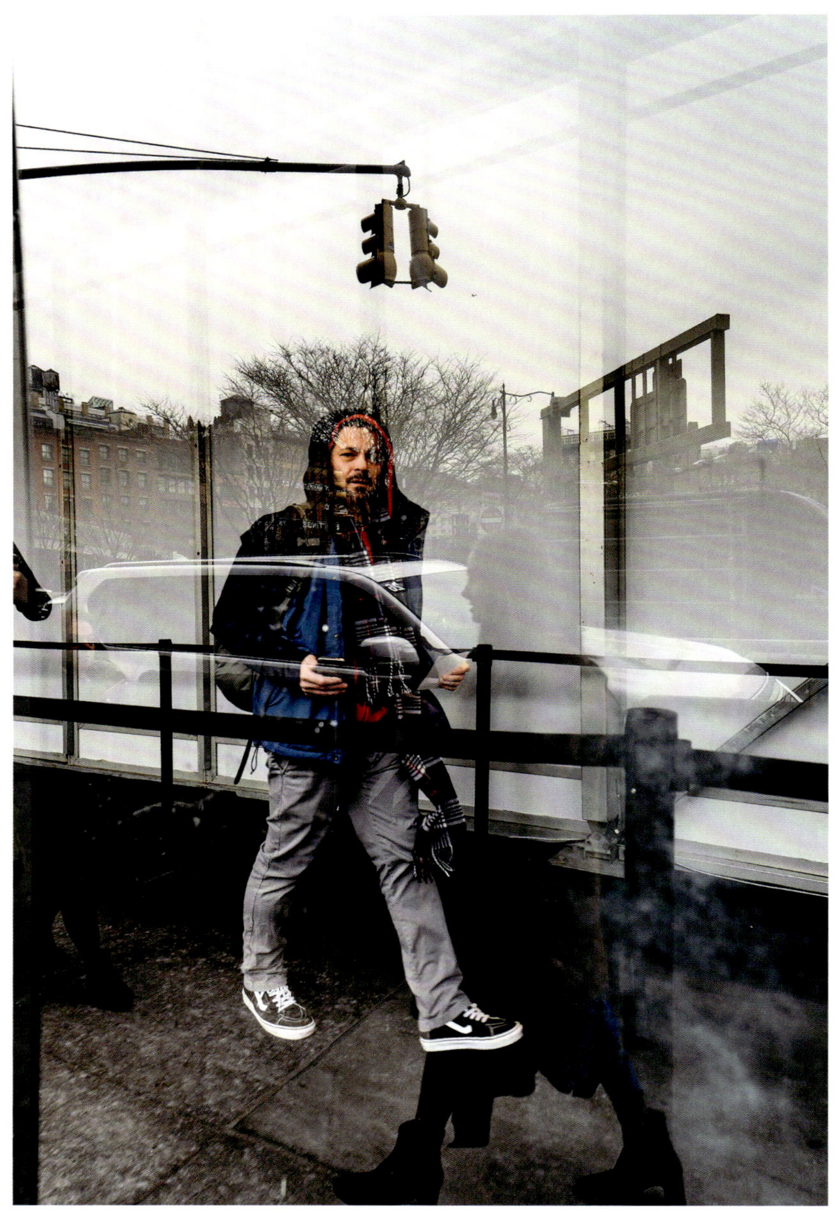

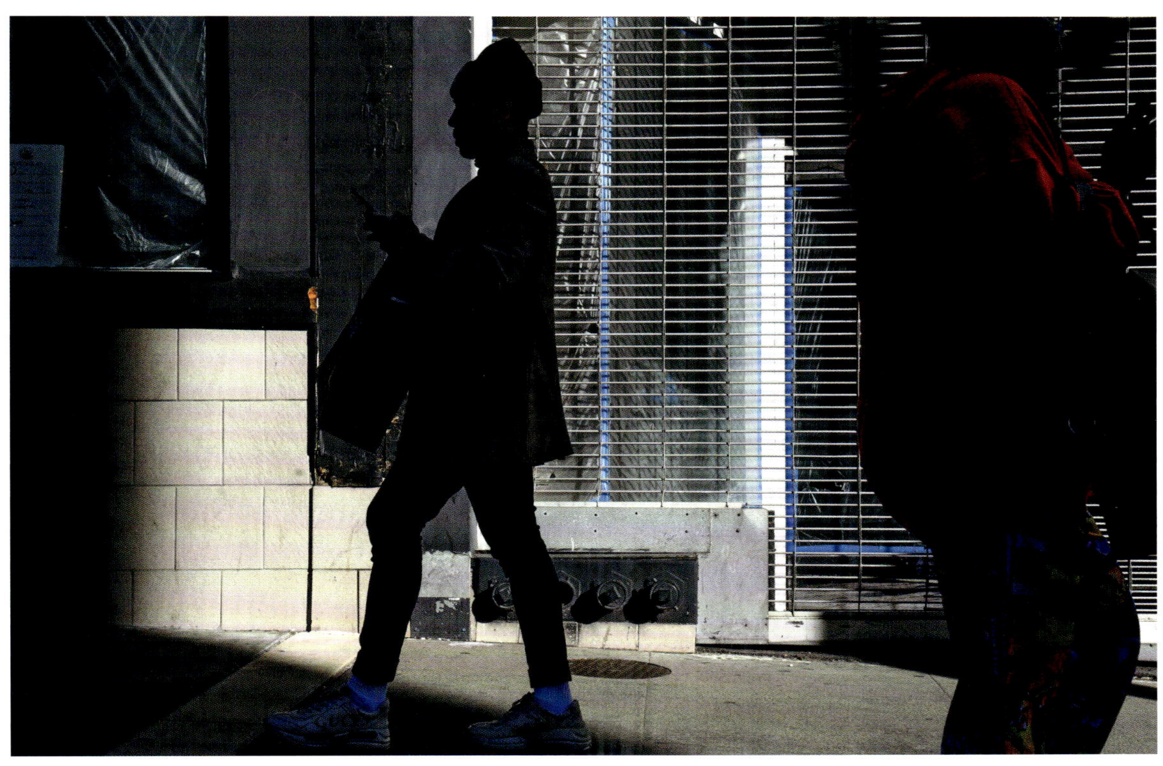

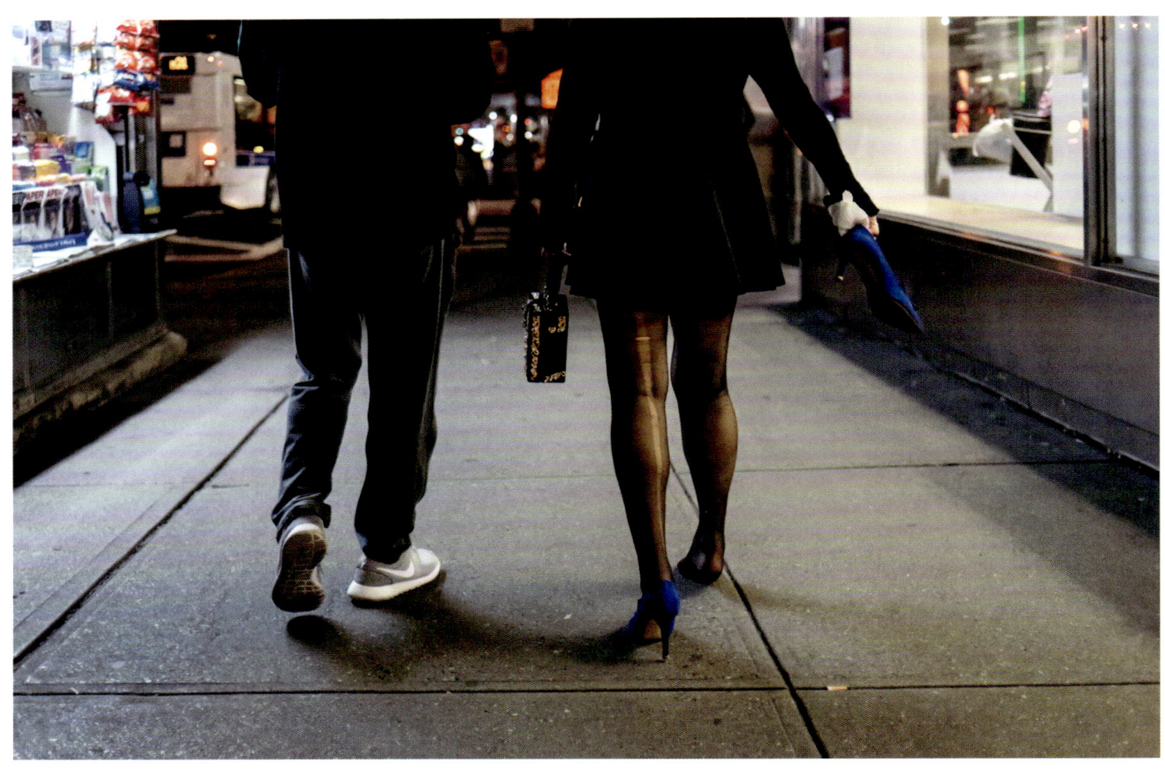

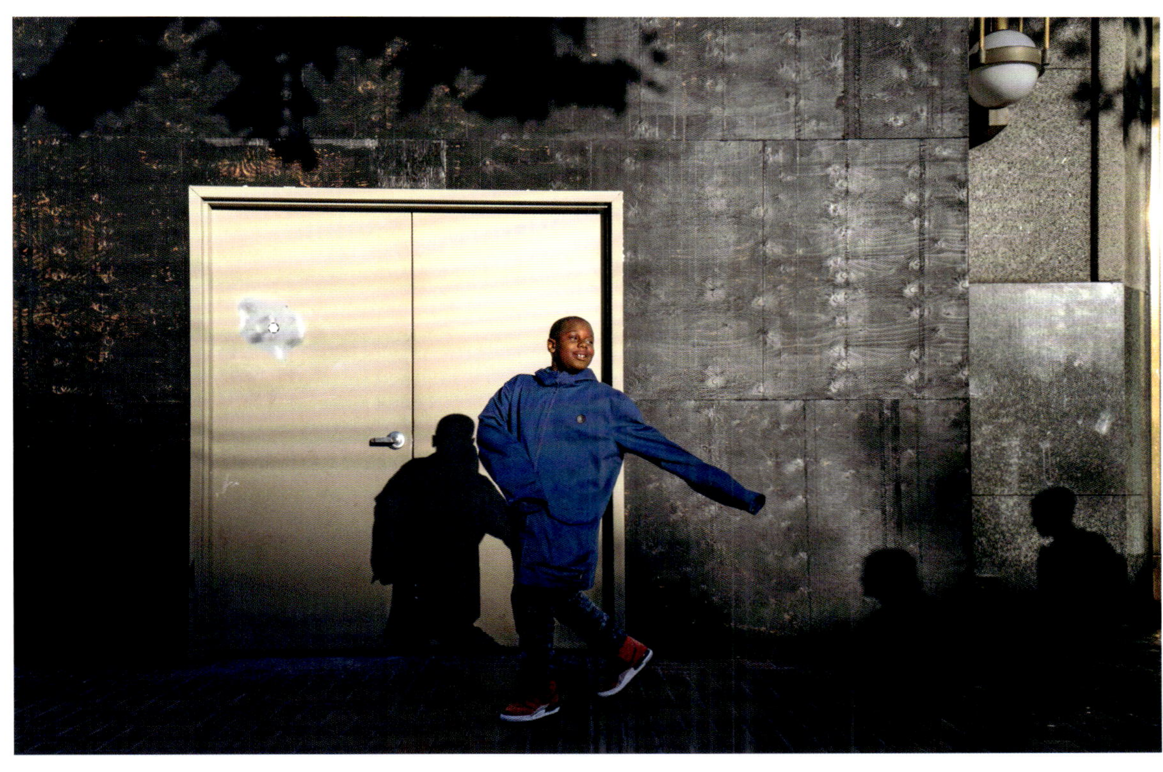

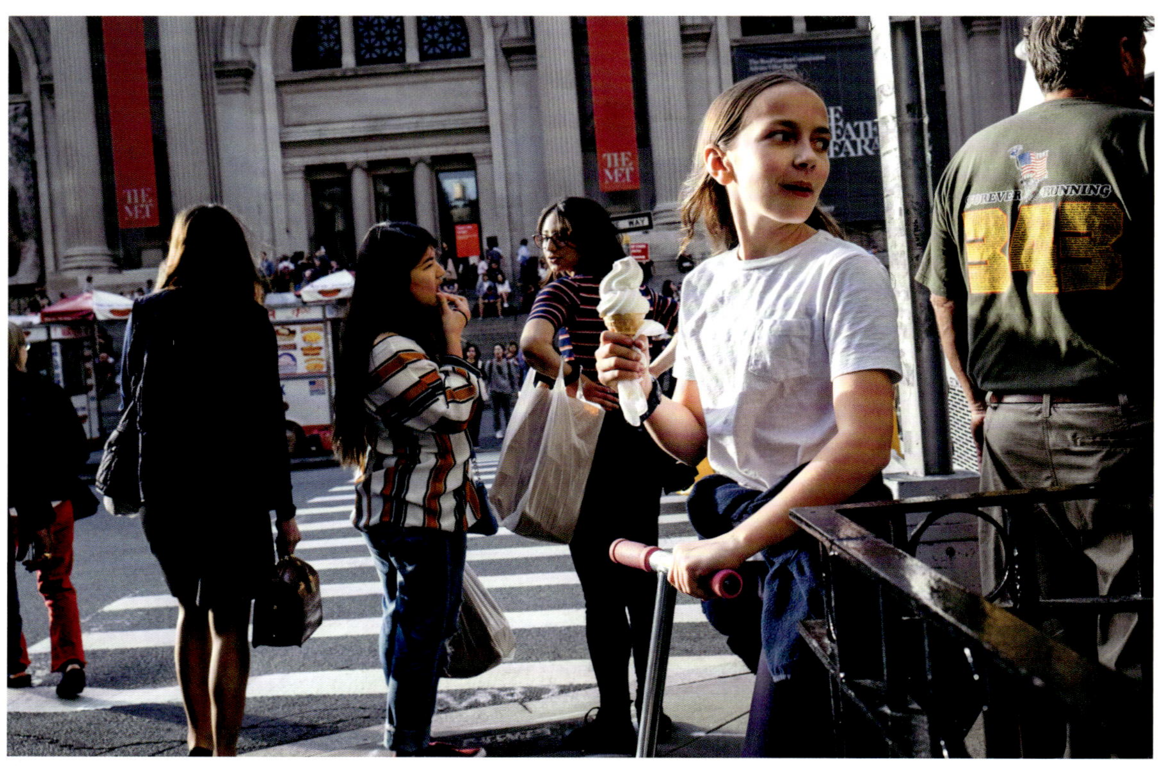

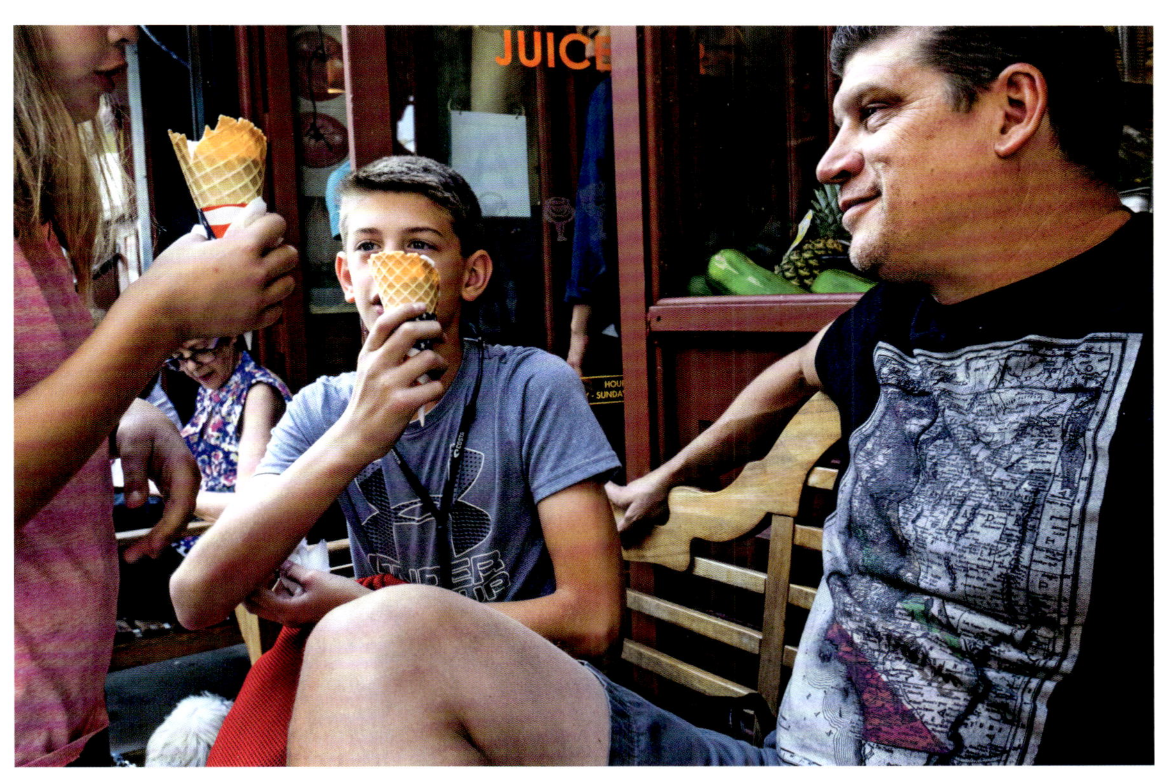

JUICE

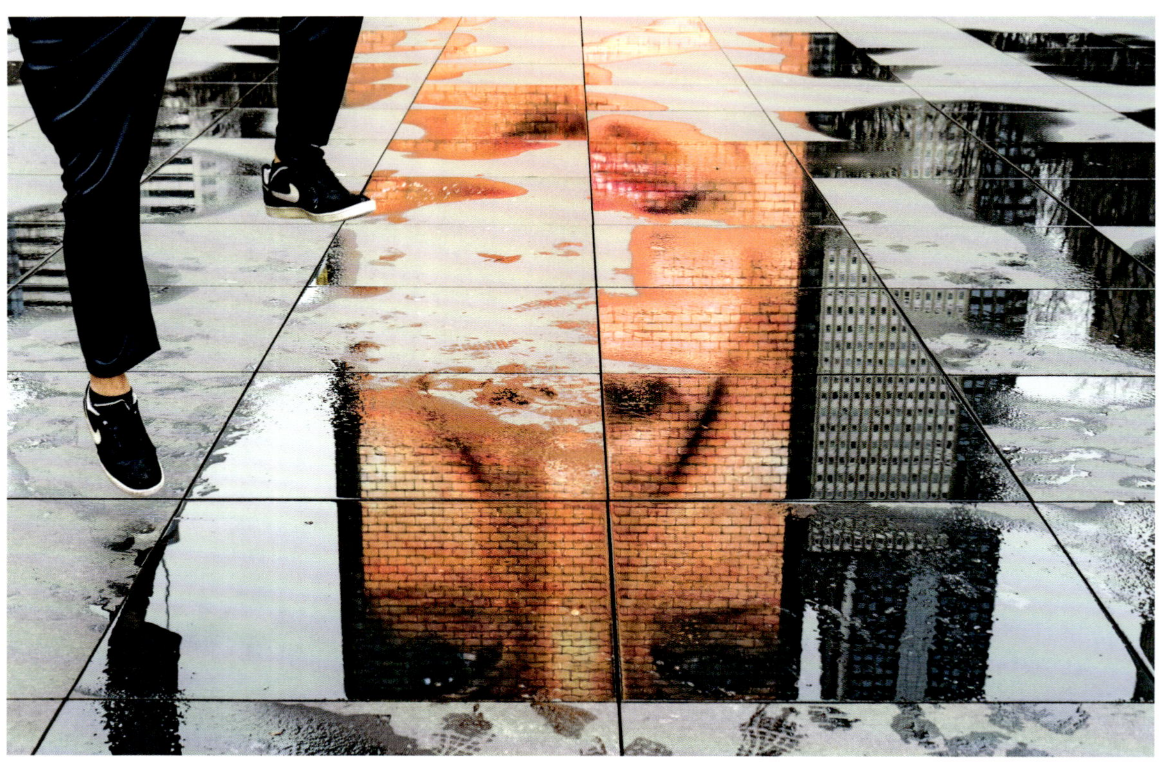

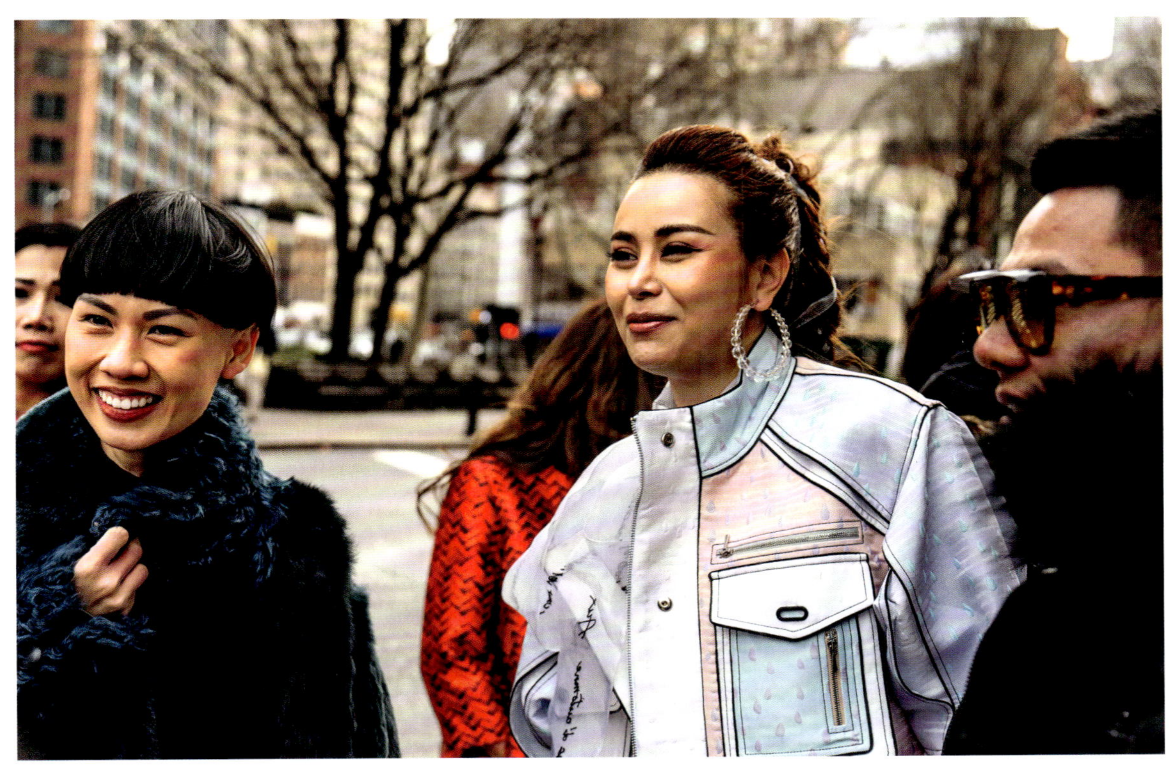

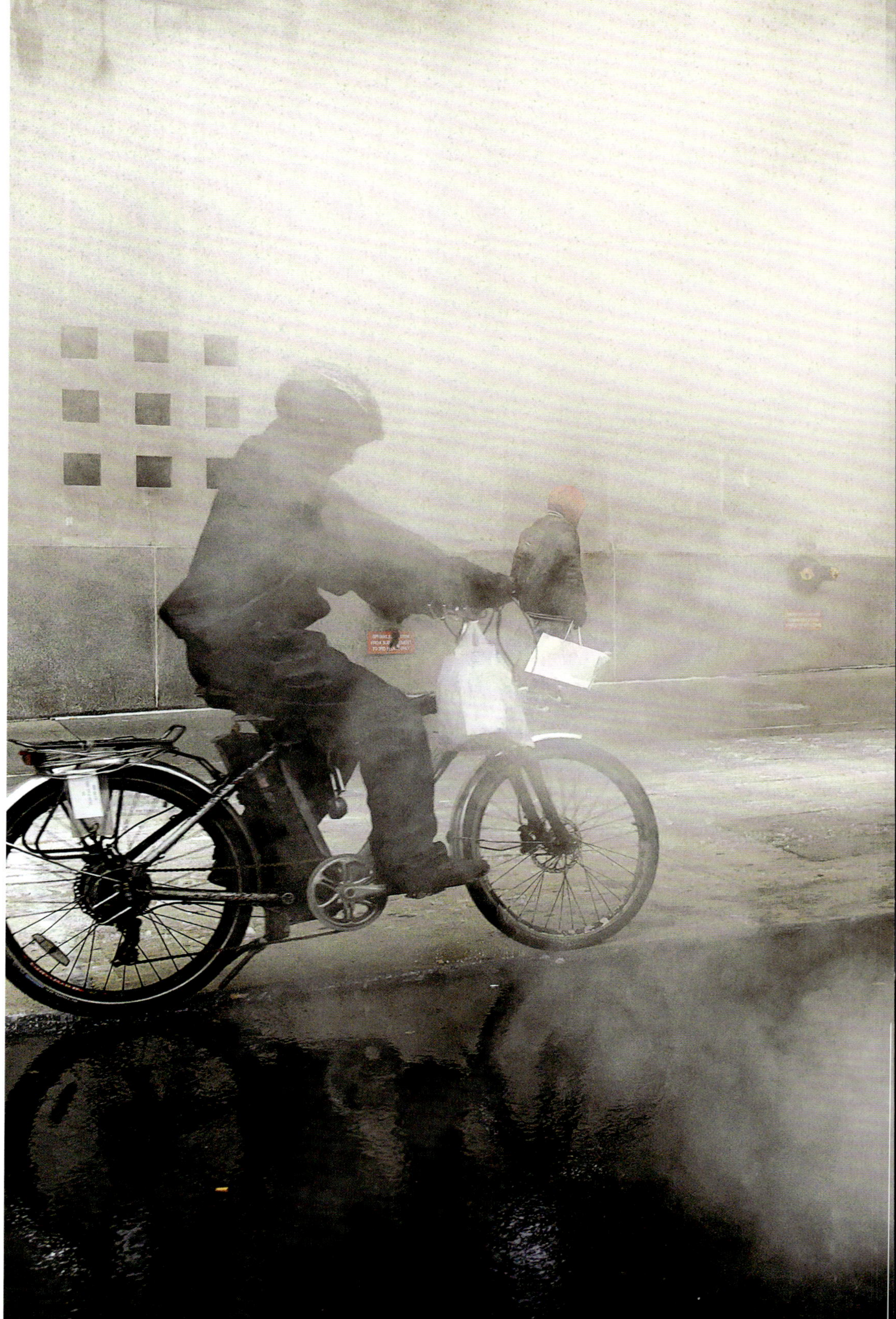

The pictures
are everywhere.
If you're open, they
will come to you.

—Jay Maisel

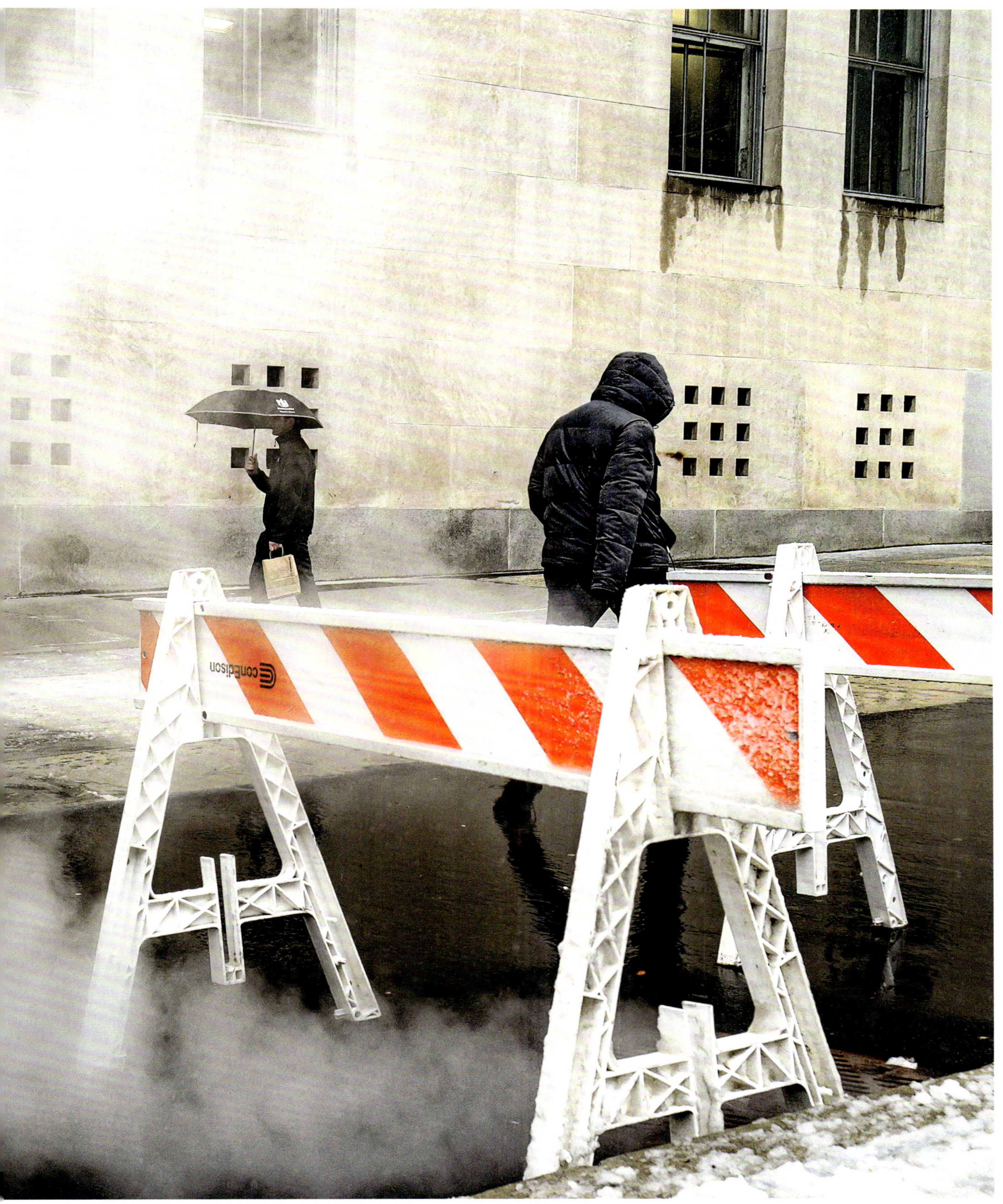
conEdison

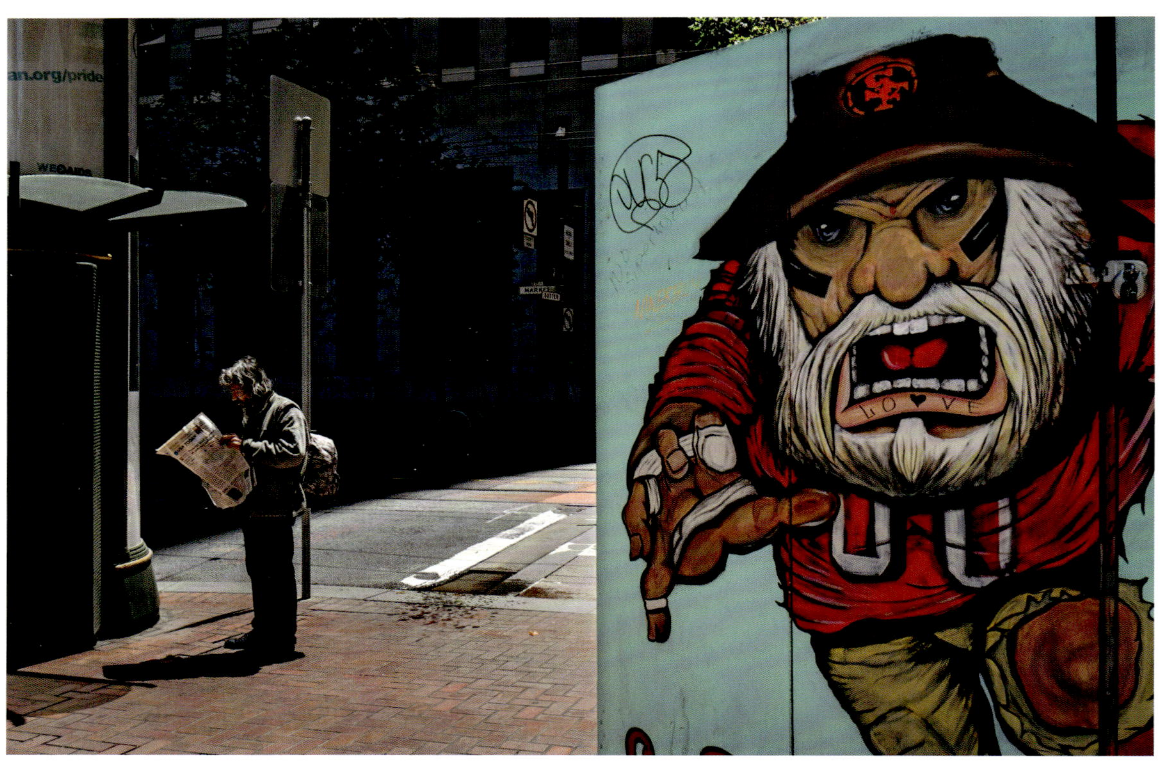
an.org/pride

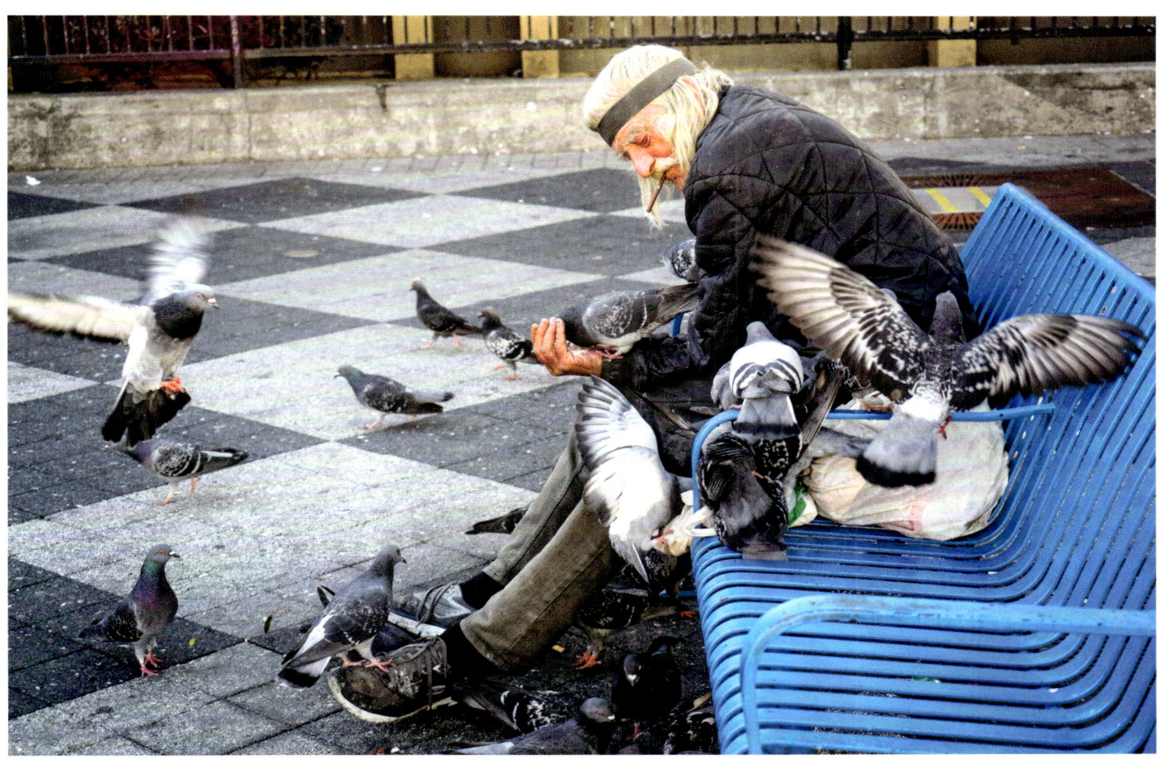

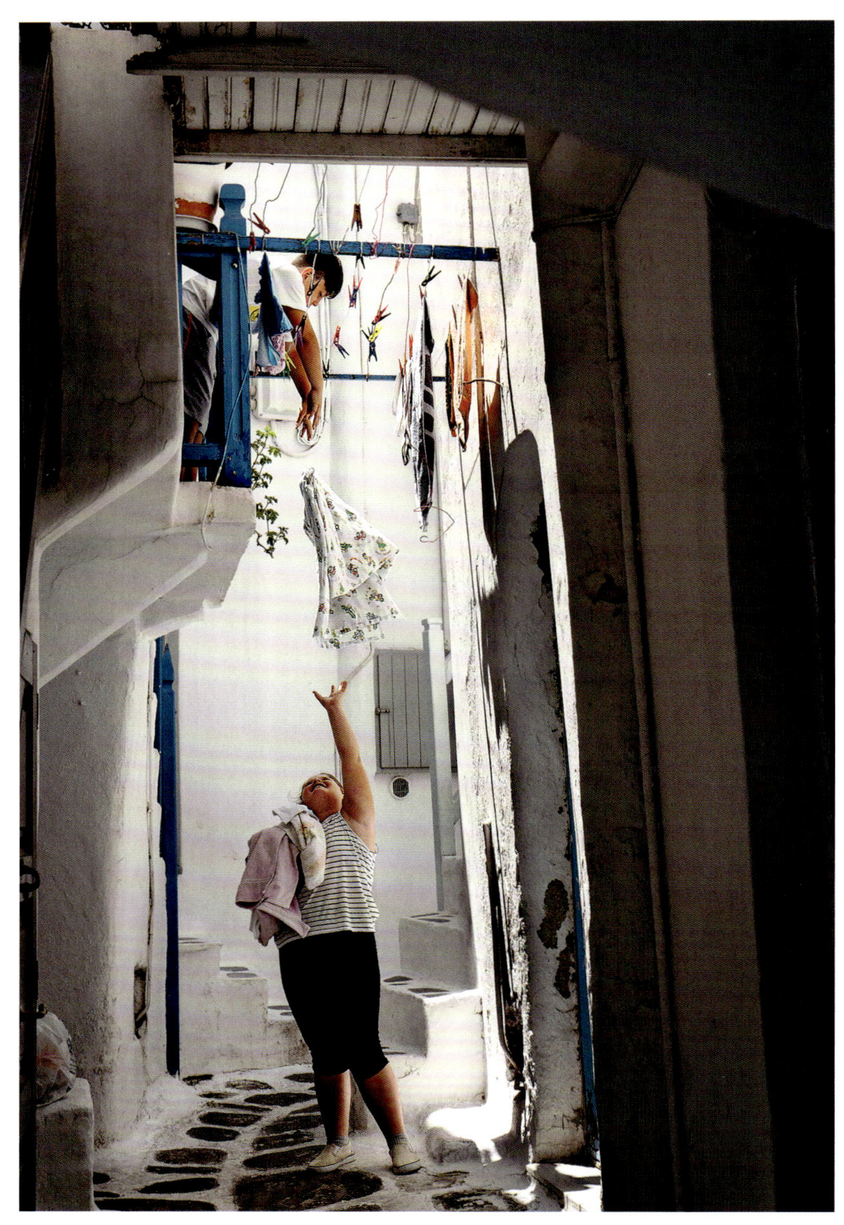

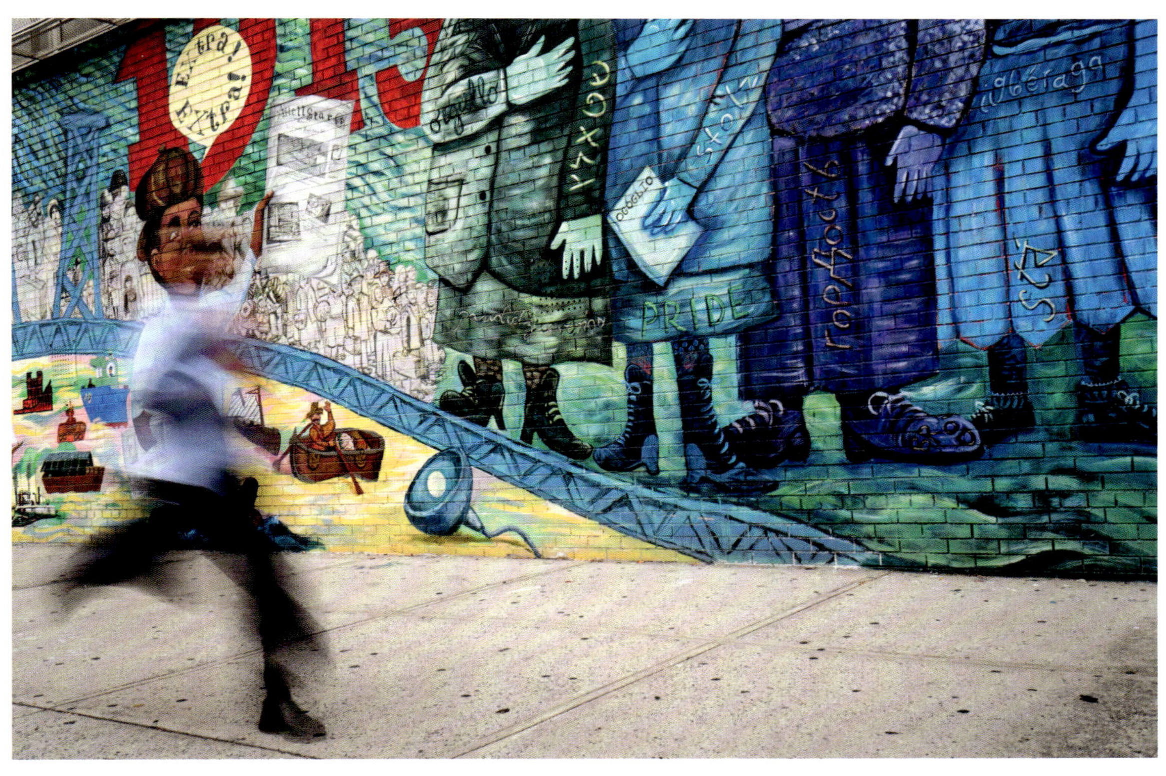

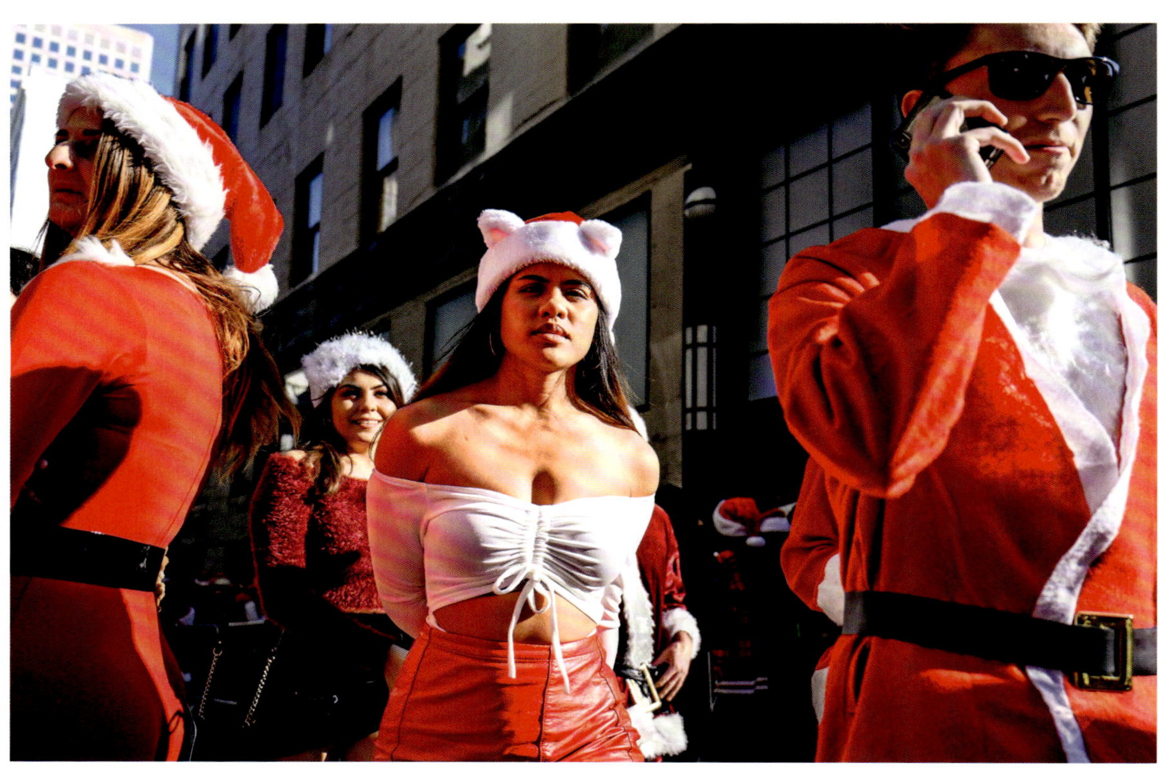

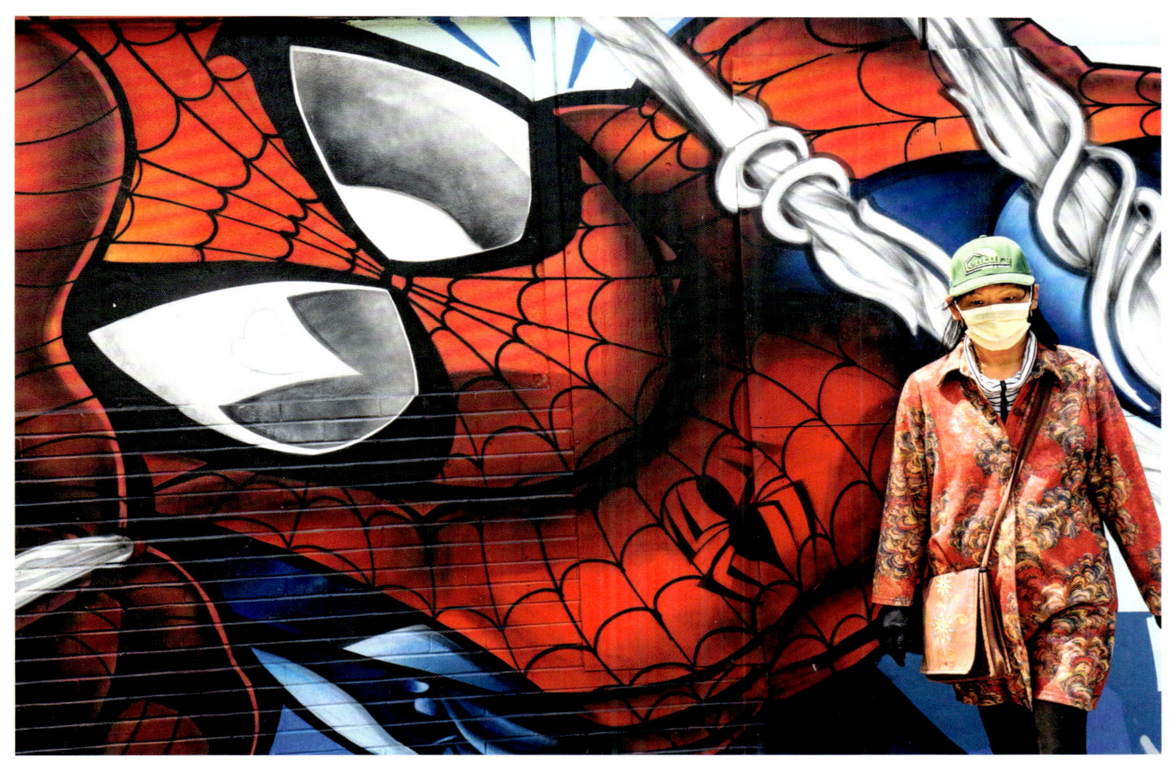

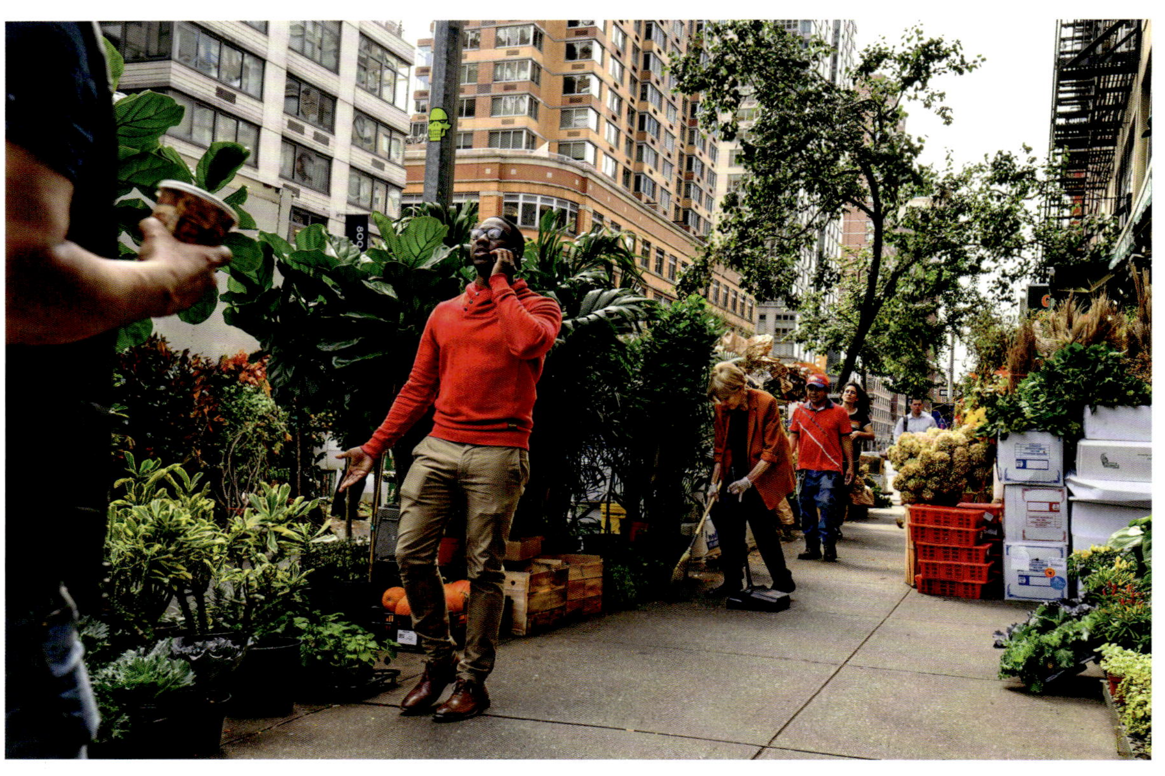

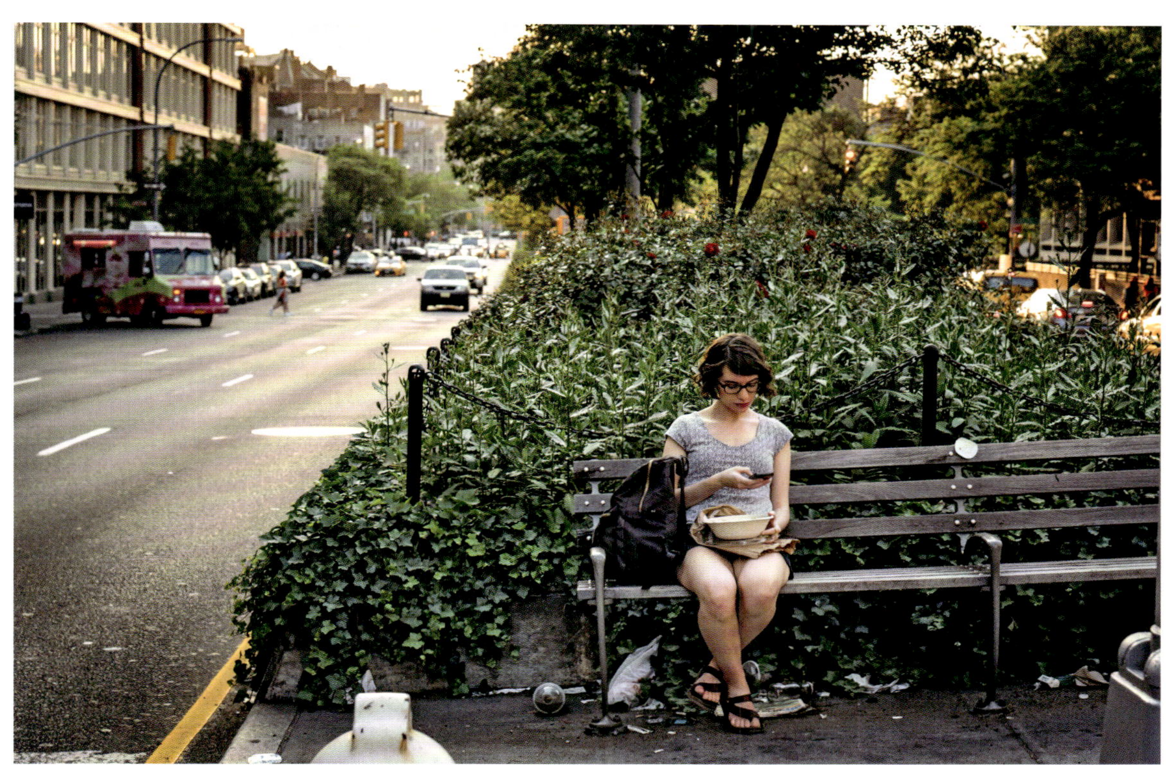

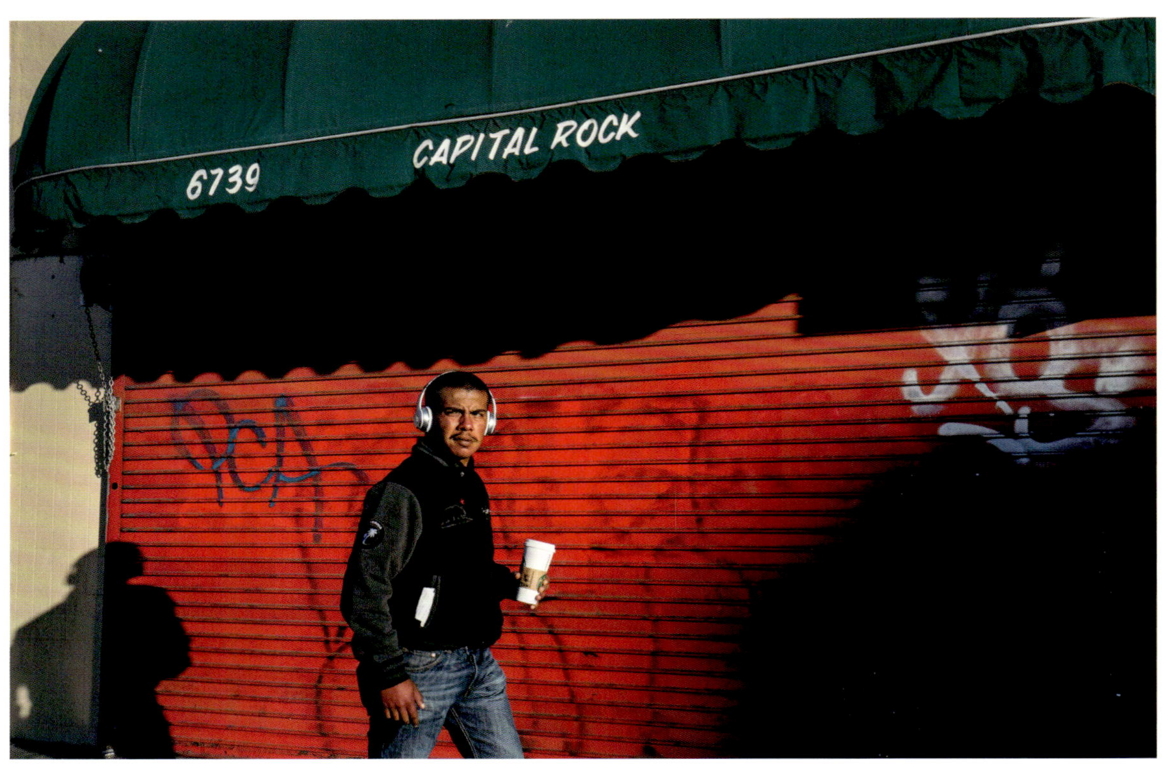

CAPITAL ROCK
6739

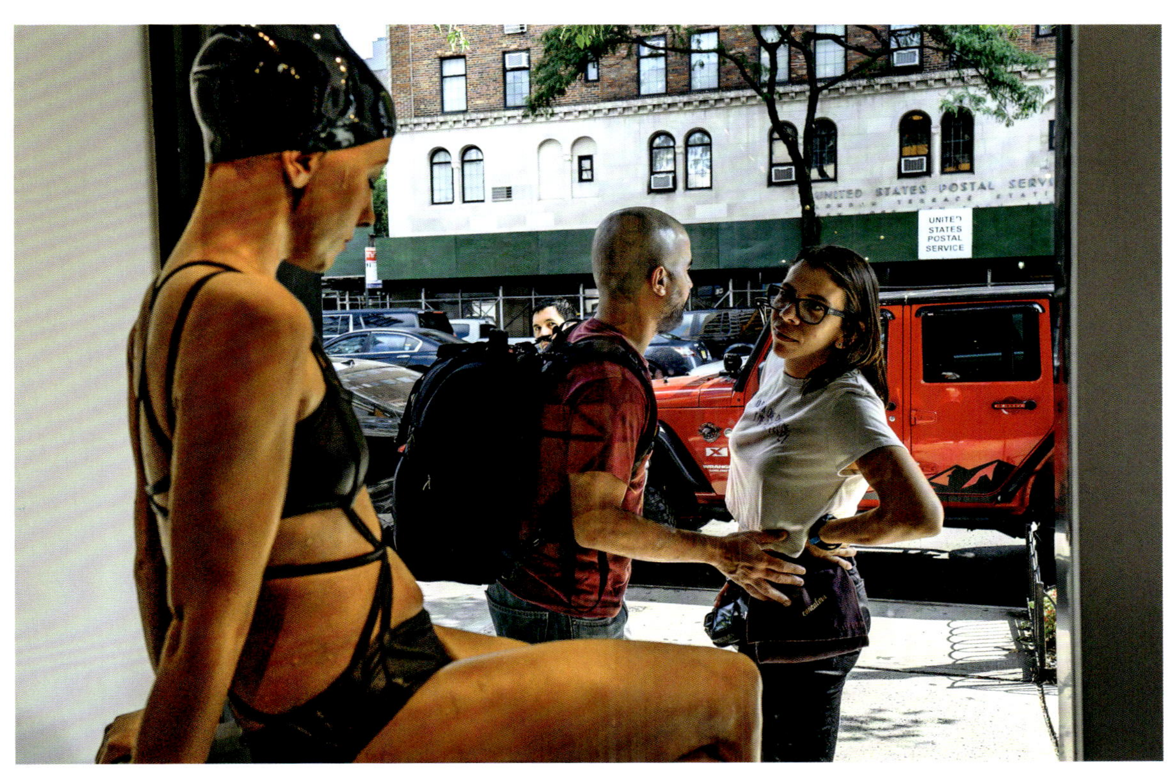

UNITED STATES POSTAL SERV
UNITED
STATES
POSTAL
SERVICE

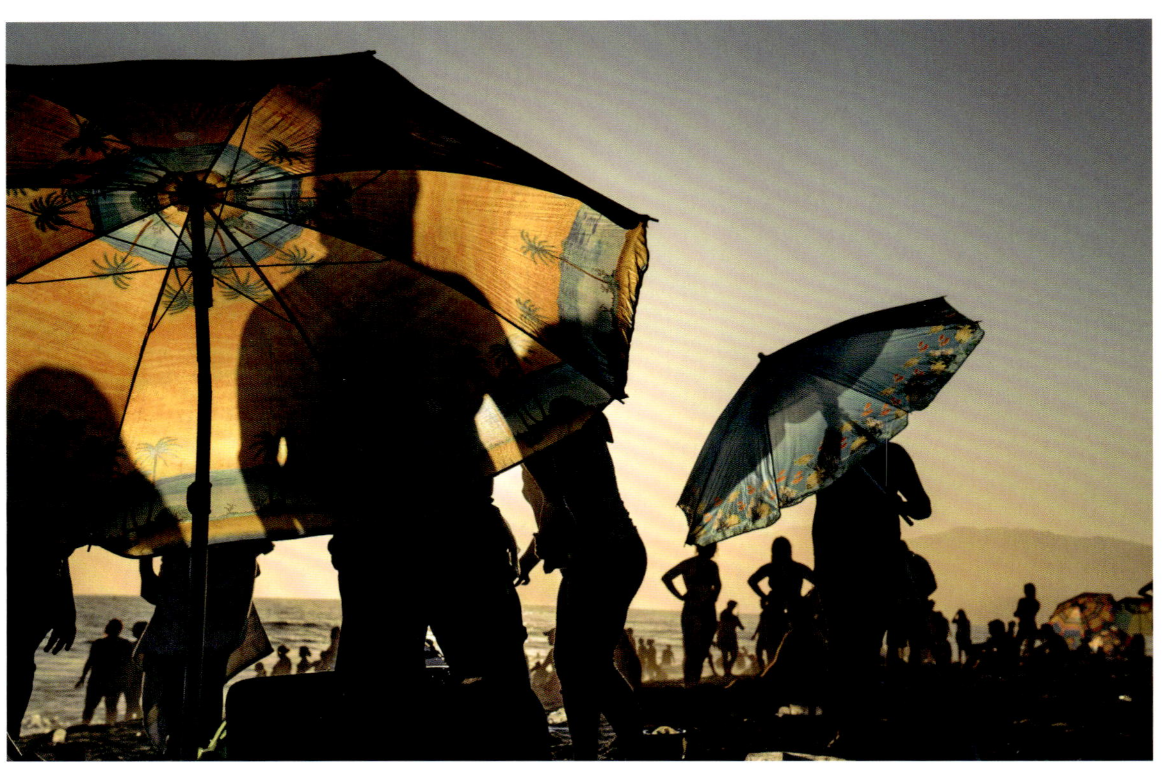

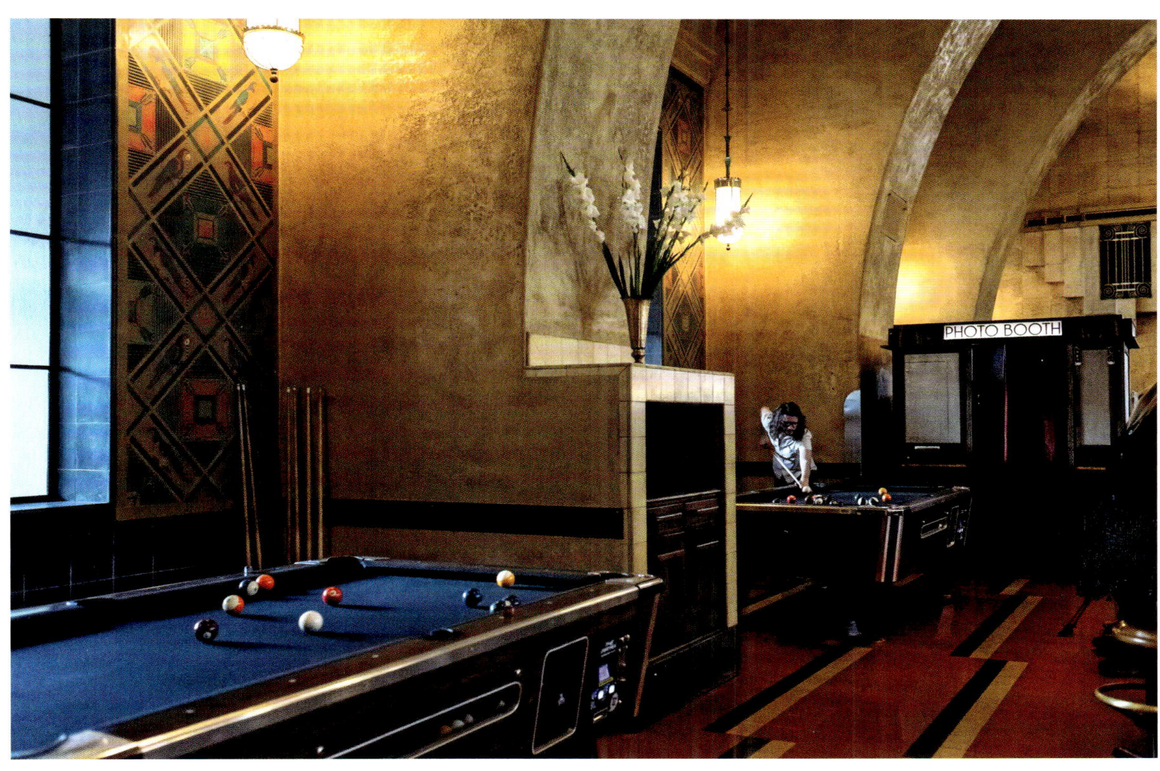
PHOTO BOOTH

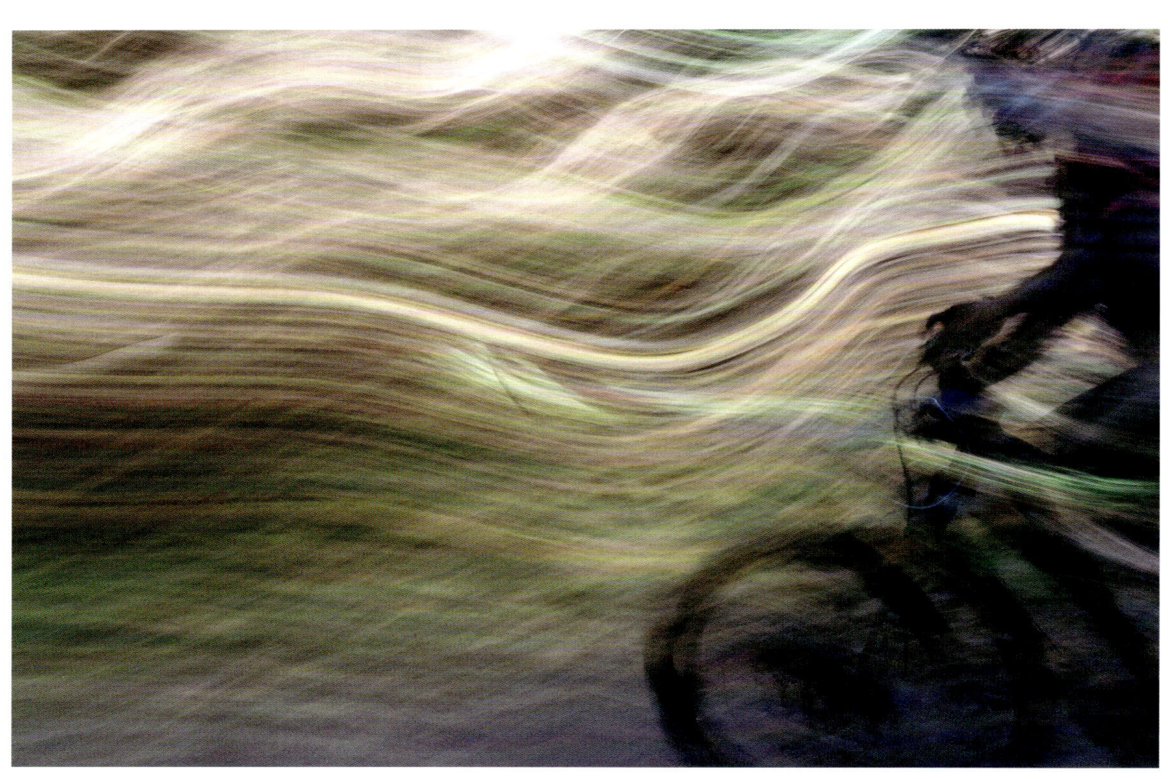

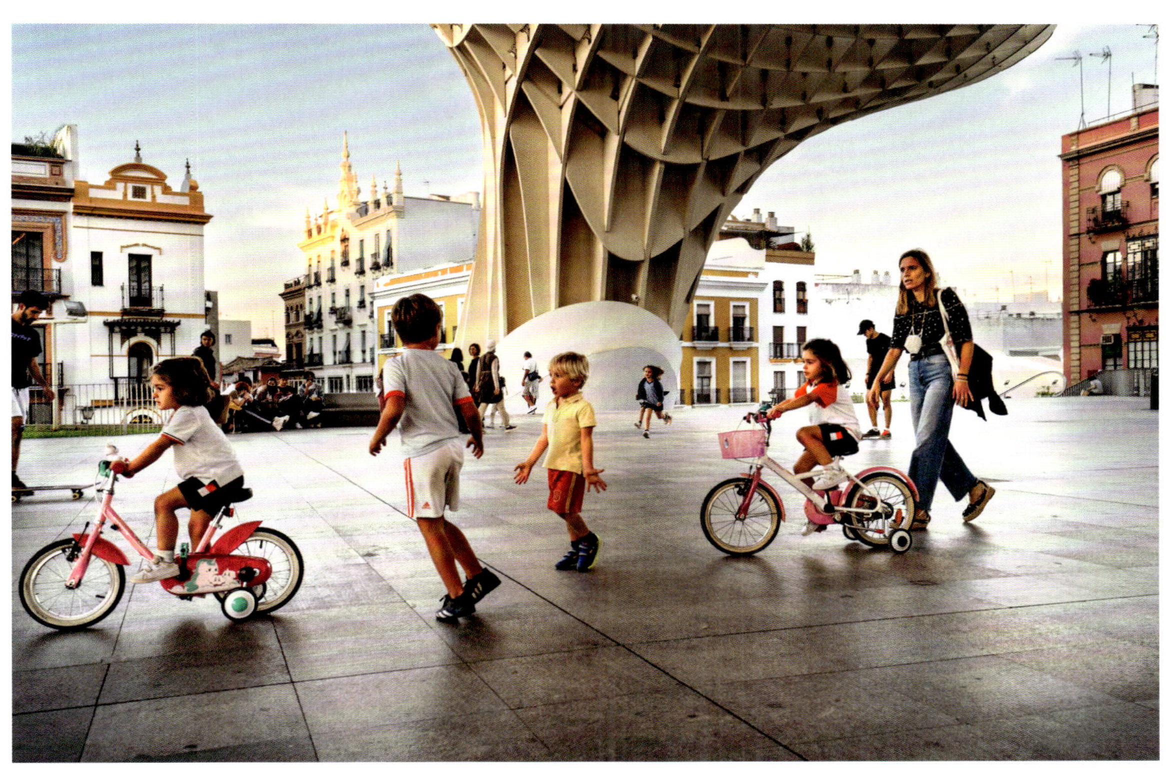

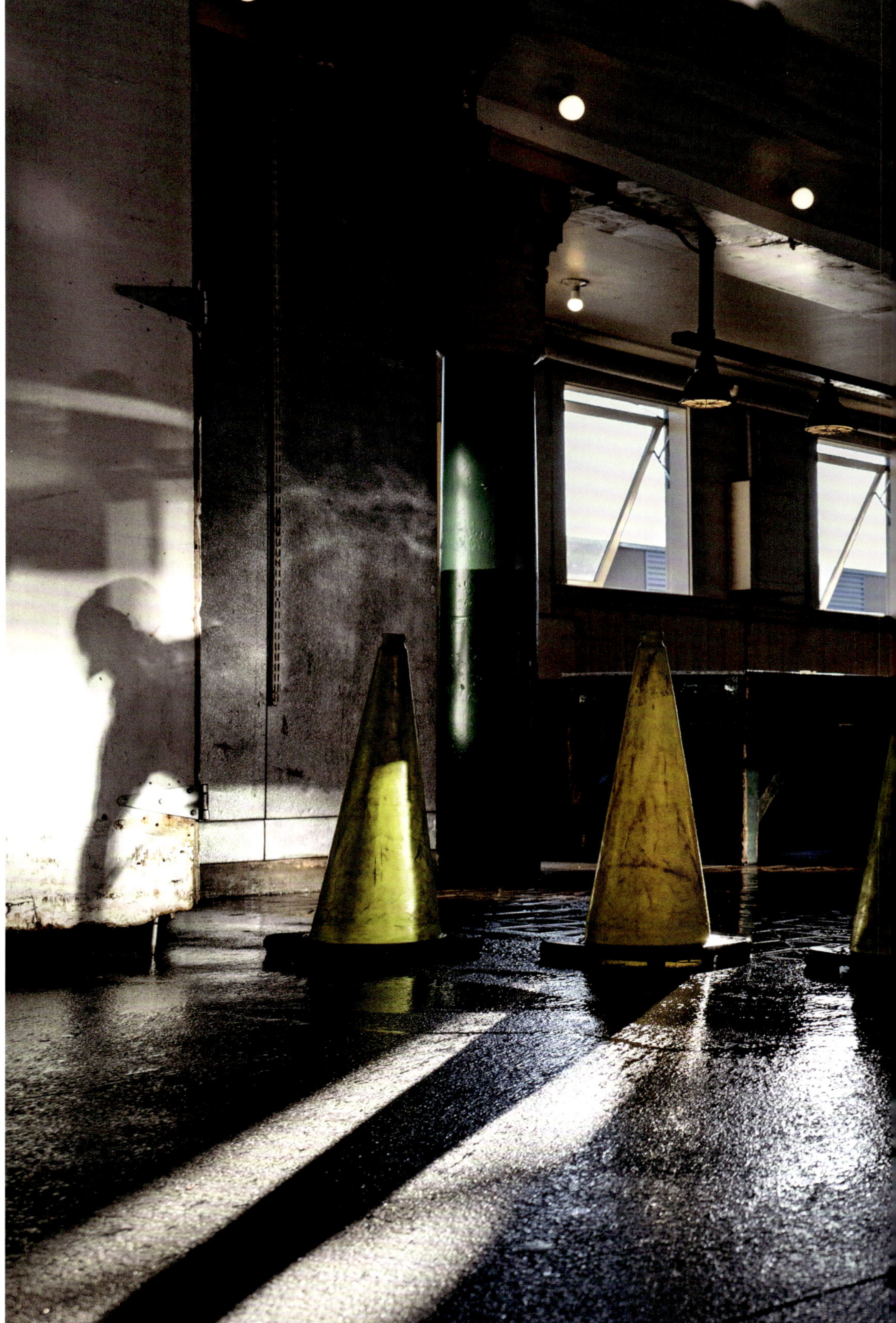

I happen to believe
in the beauty of
simple things.
I believe the most
uninteresting
things can be very
interesting.

—Saul Leiter

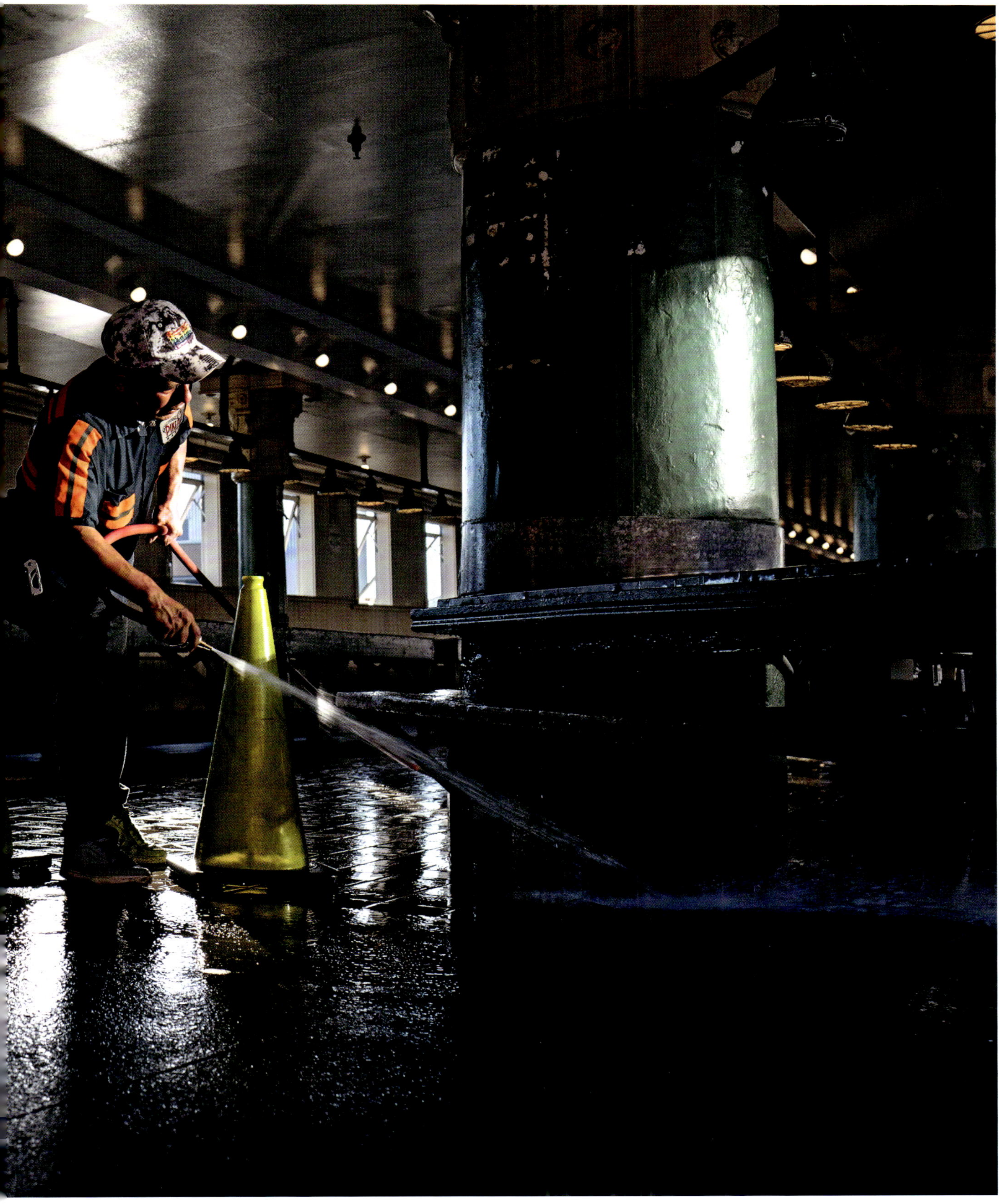

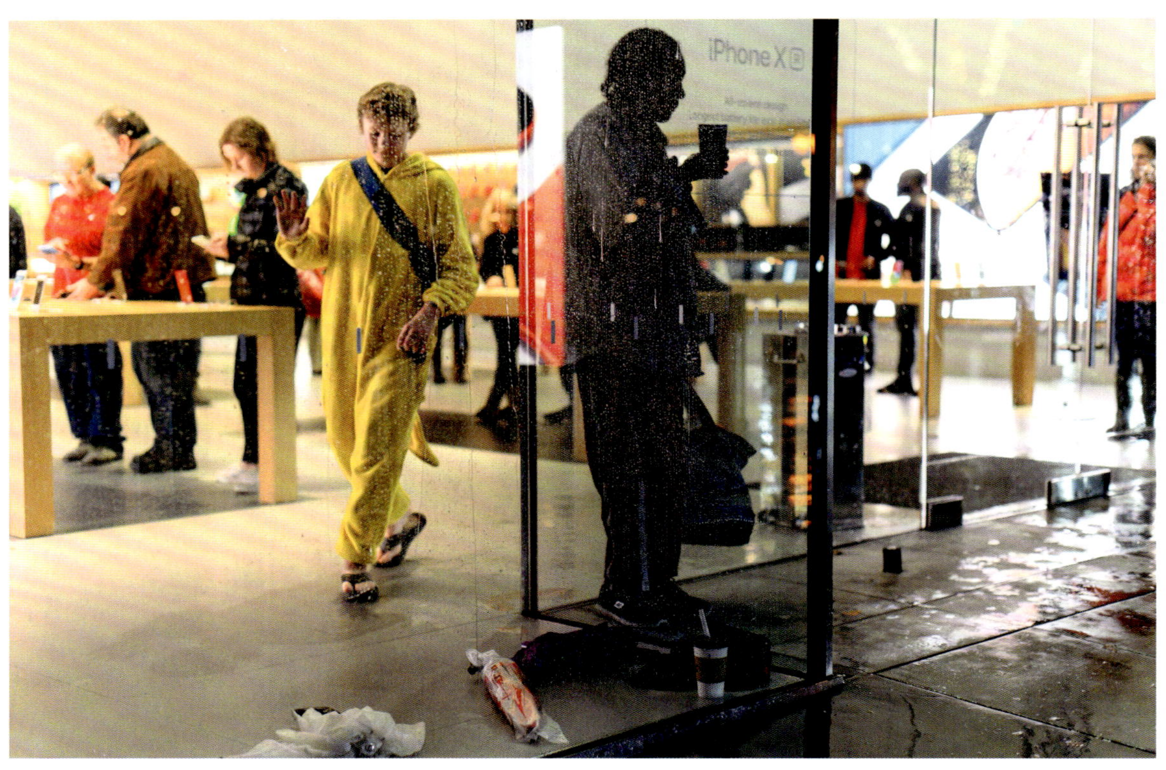

iPhone X

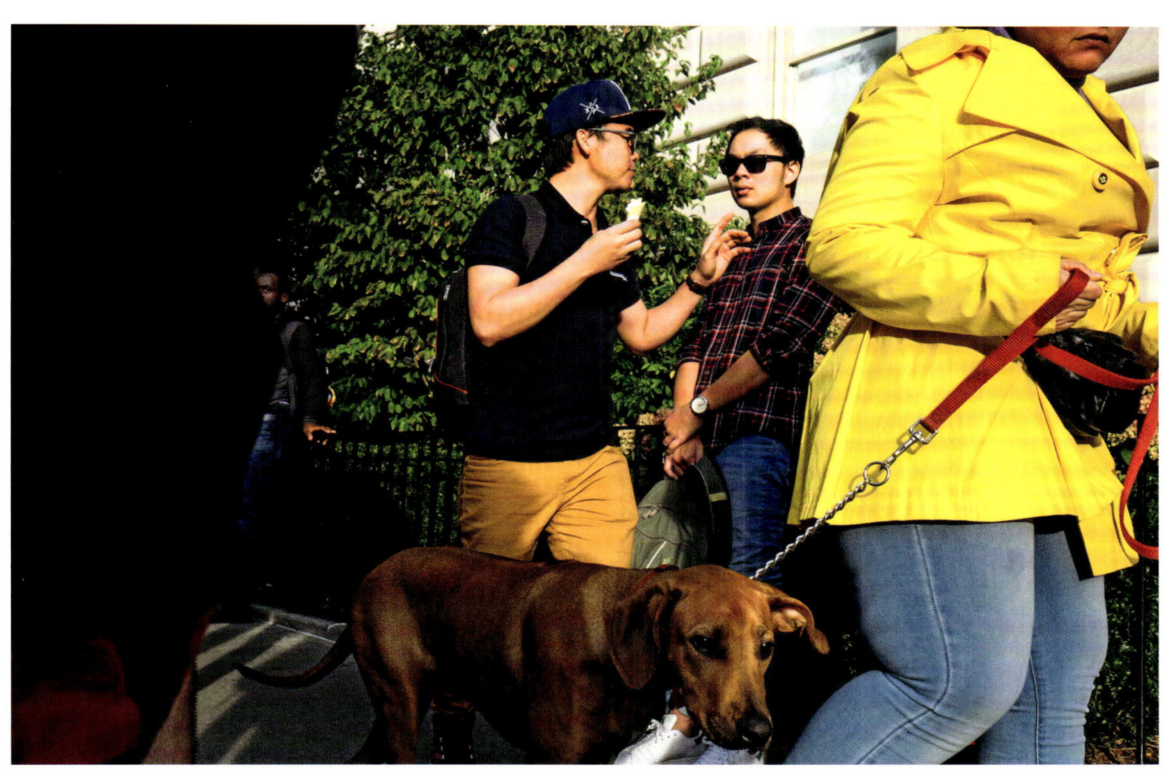

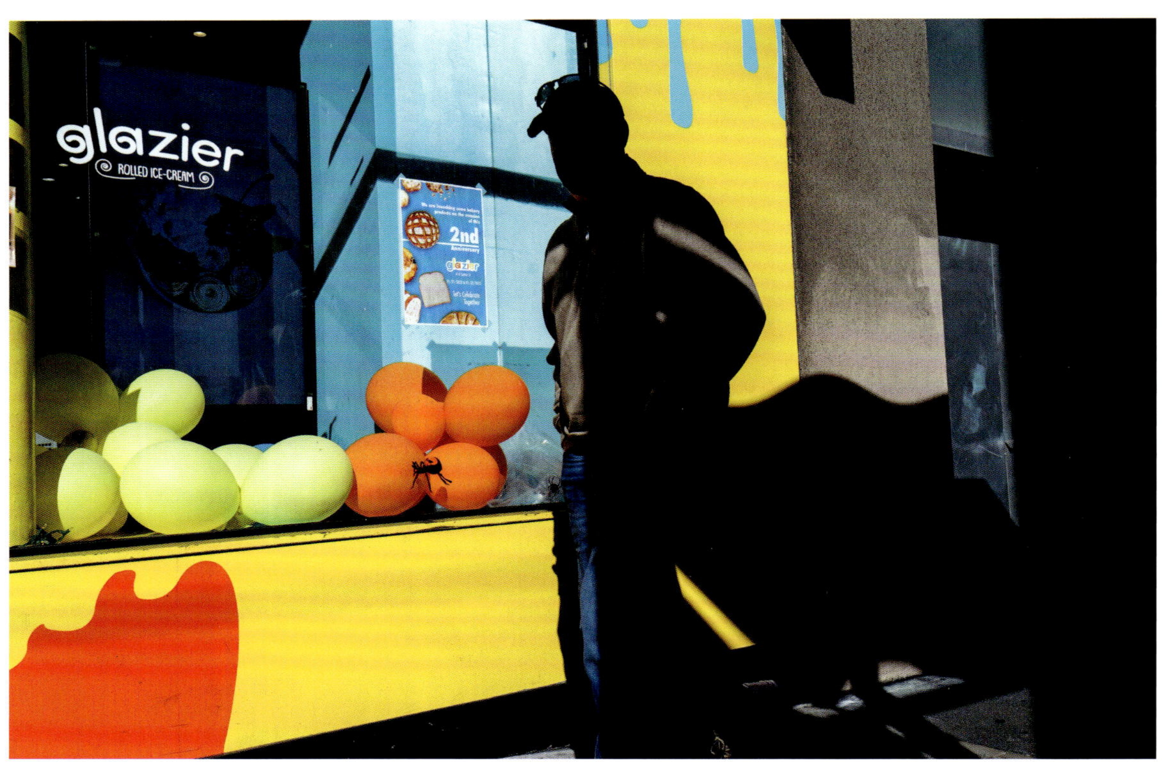
glazier
ROLLED ICE-CREAM
2nd
glazier

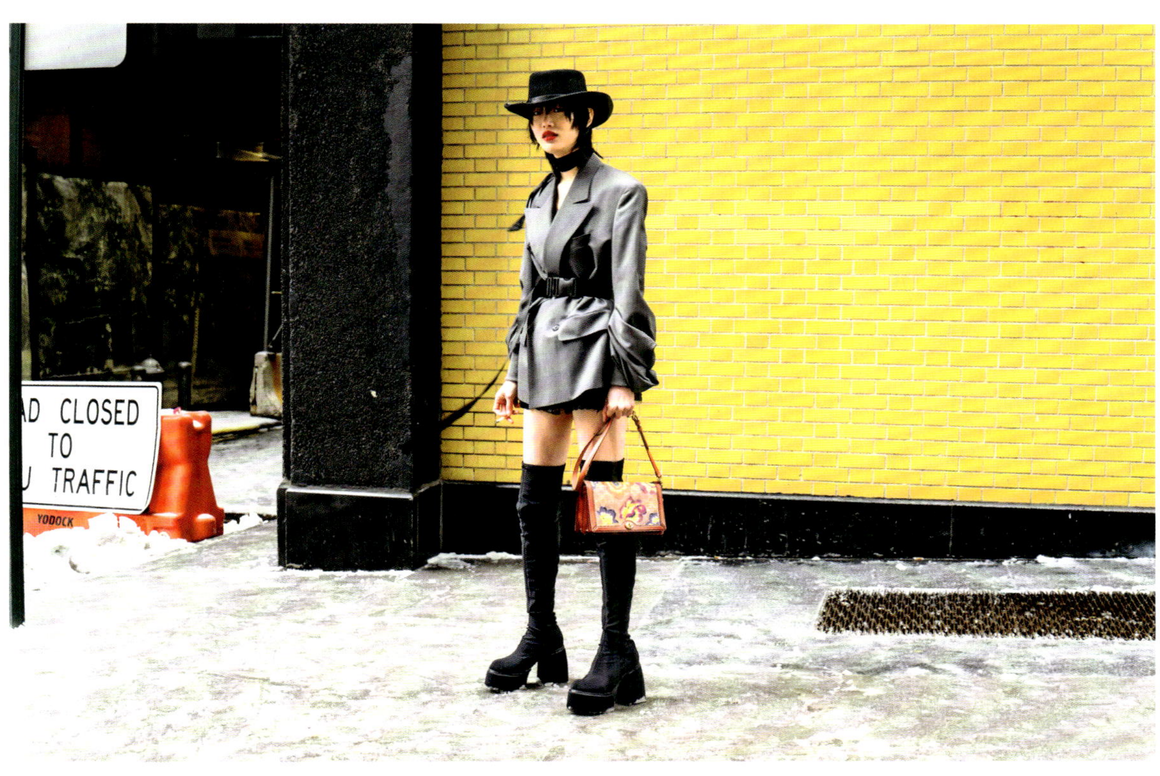
AD CLOSED
TO
U TRAFFIC
YODOCK

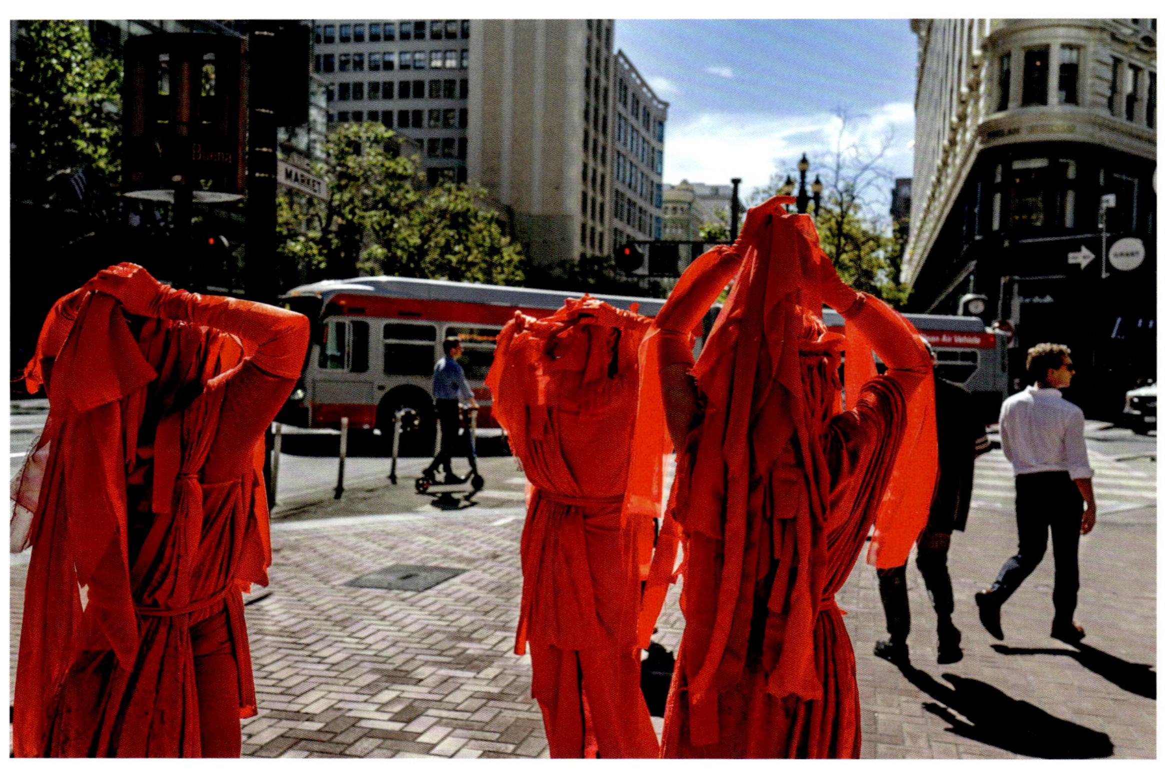

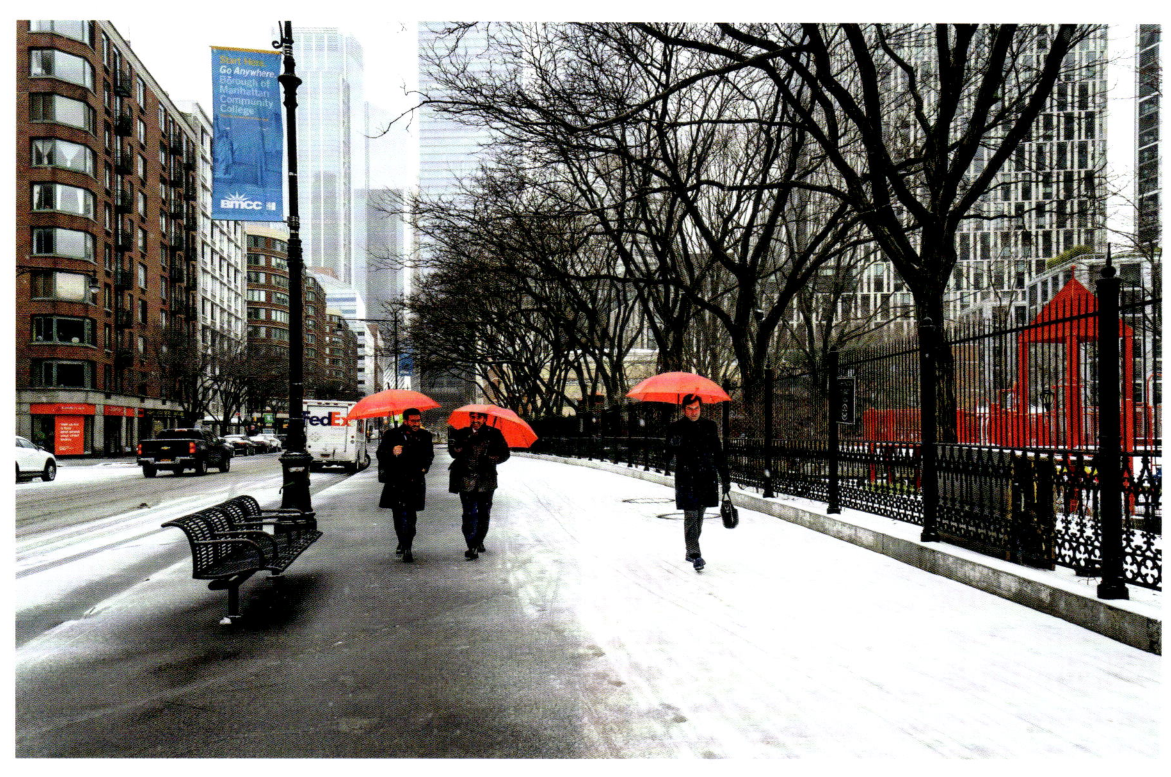

Start Here
Go Anywhere
Borough of
Manhattan
Community
College
BMCC
FedEx

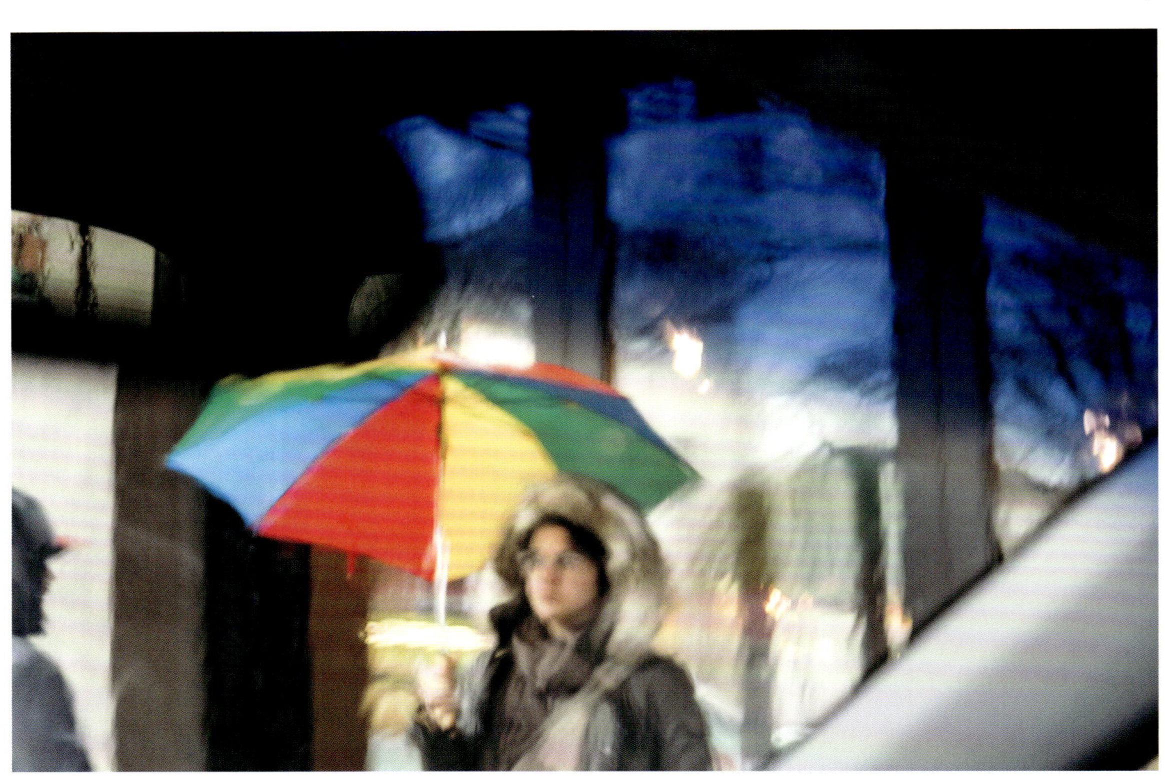

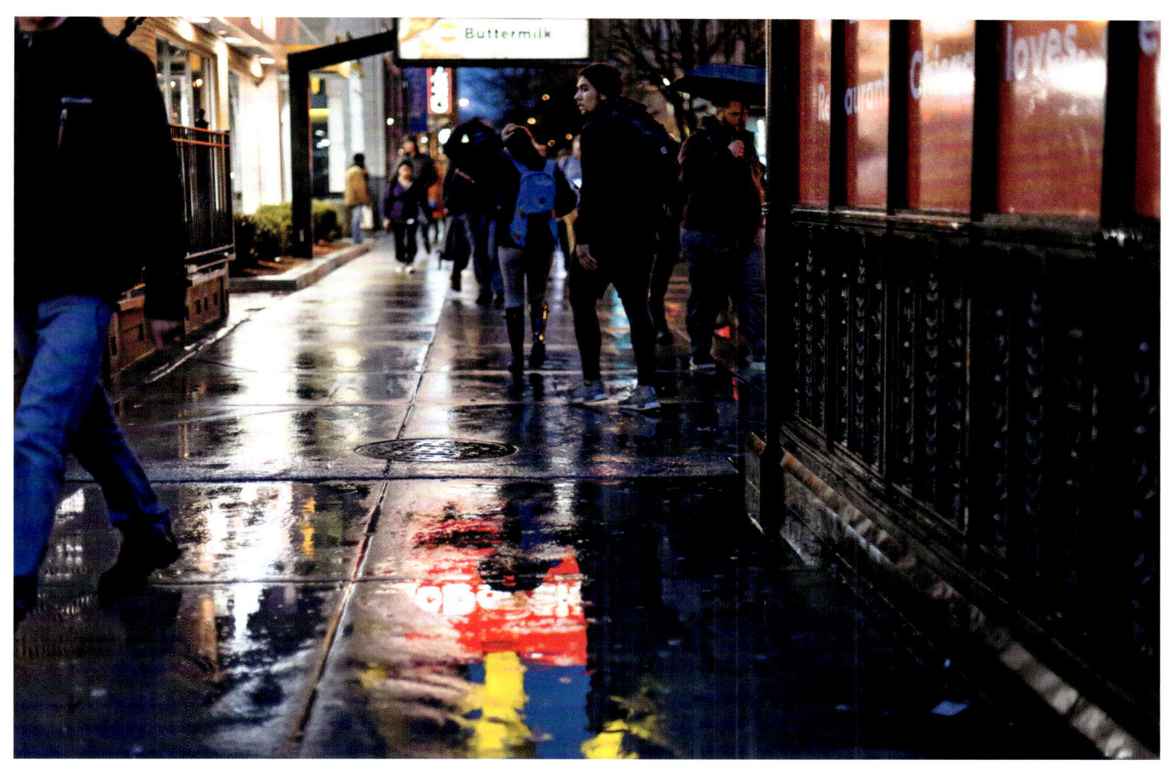
Buttermilk
Restaurant

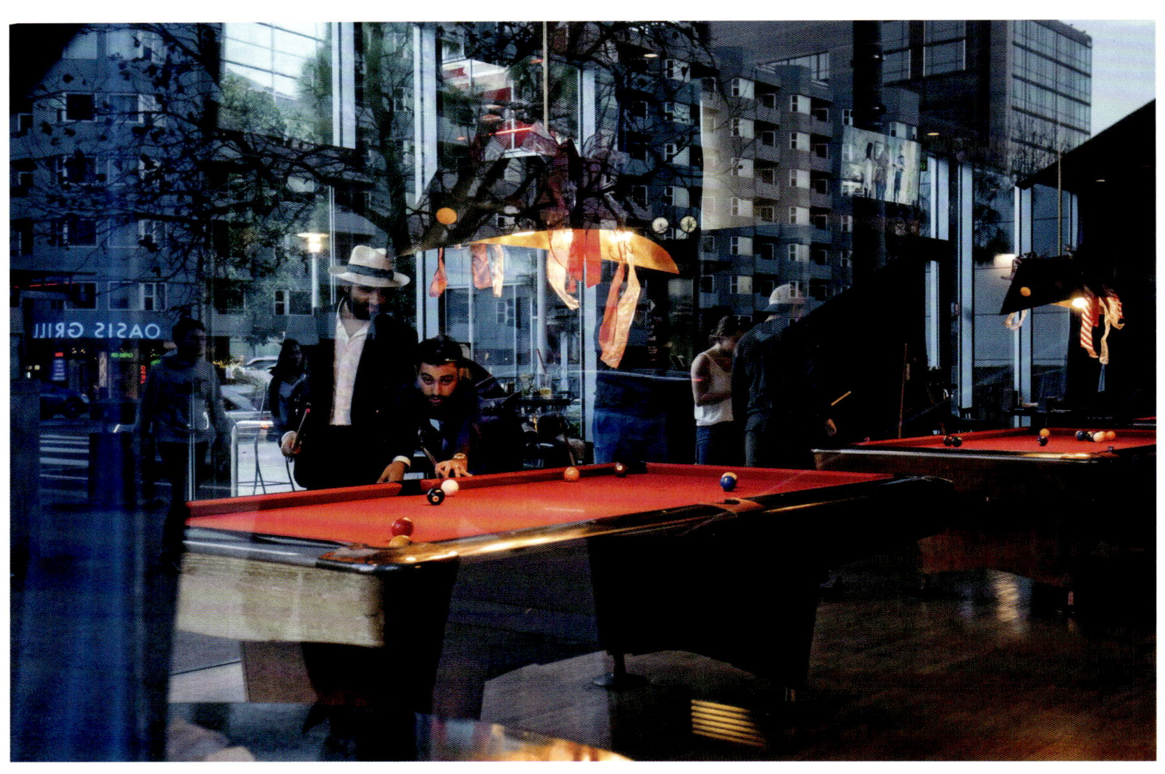

OASIS GRILL

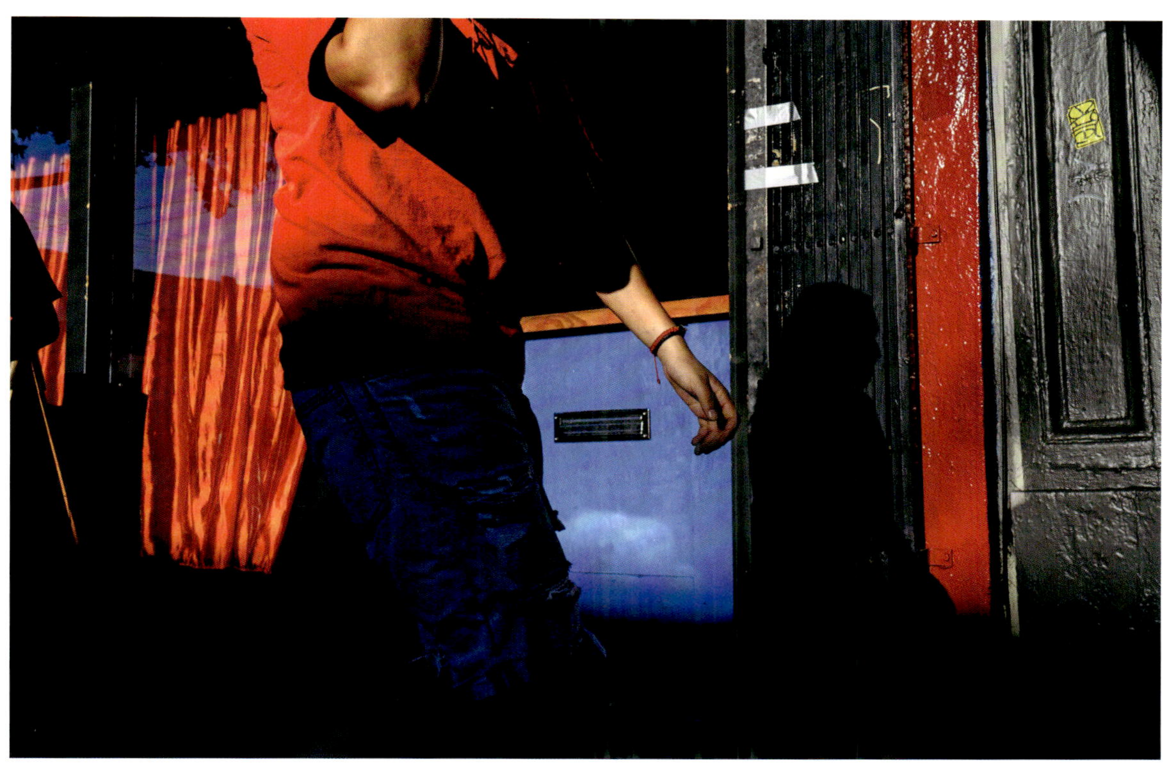

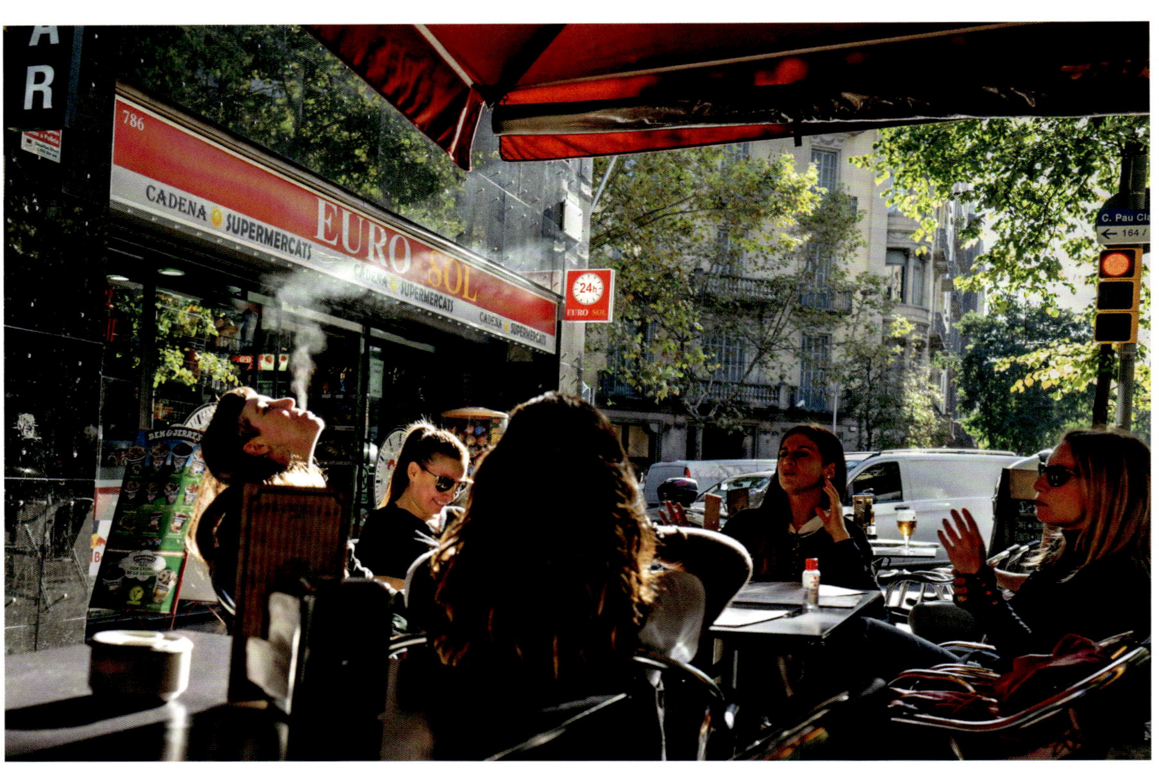
AR
786
CADENA SUPERMERCATS
EURO SOL
CADENA SUPERMERCATS
24h
EURO SOL
C. Pau Cla
164 /
BEN&JERRY'S

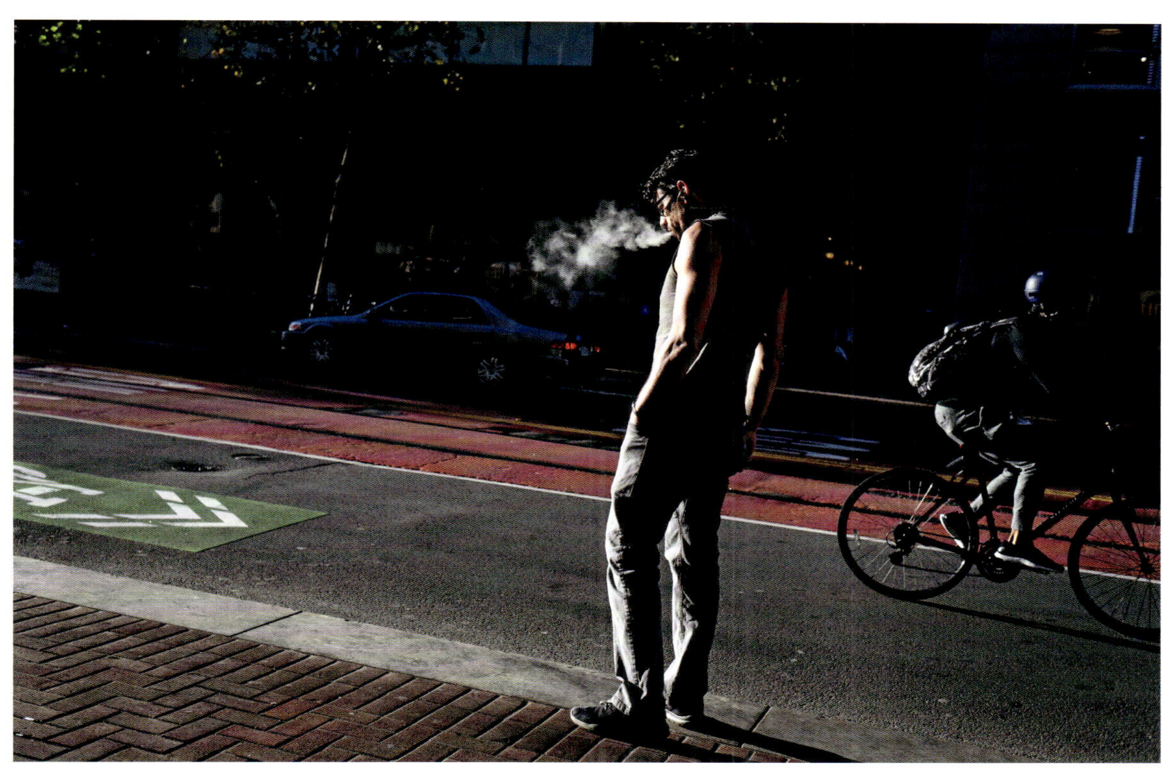

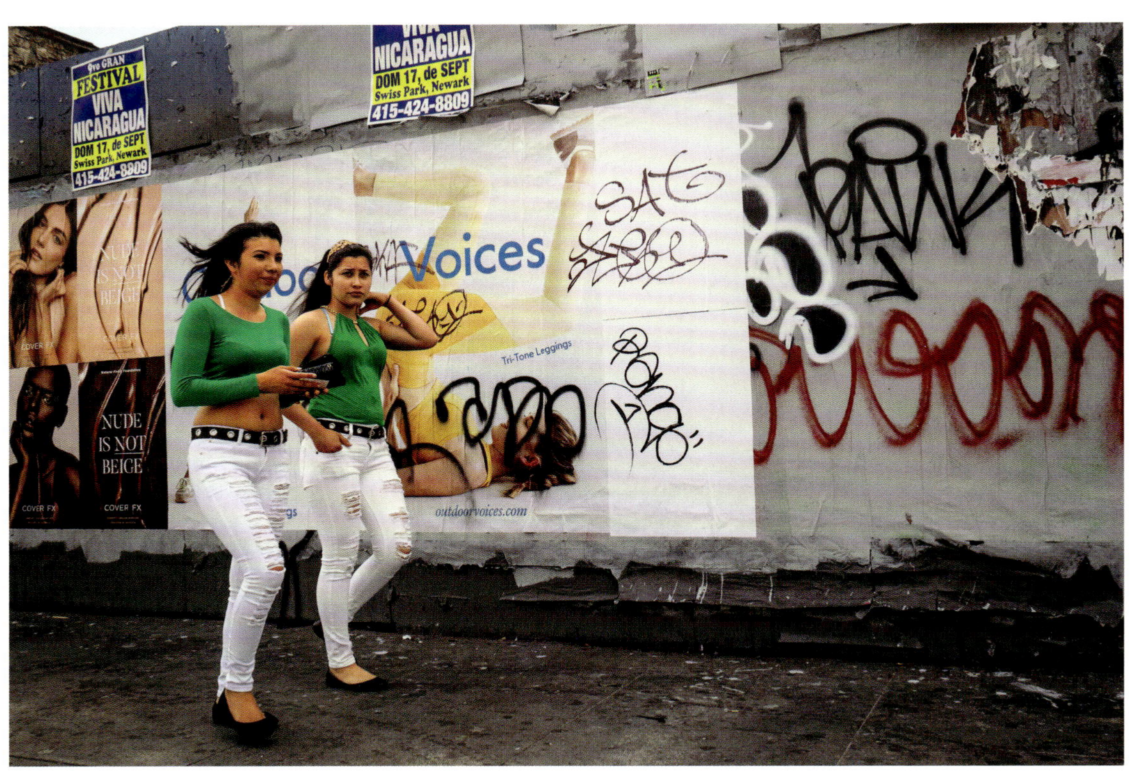
9na GRAN
FESTIVAL
VIVA
NICARAGUA
DOM 17, de SEPT
Swiss Park, Newark
415-424-8809
VIVA
NICARAGUA
DOM 17, de SEPT
Swiss Park, Newark
415-424-8809
Voices
Tri-Tone Leggings
outdoorvoices.com
NUDE
IS NOT
BEIGE
COVER FX
COVER FX

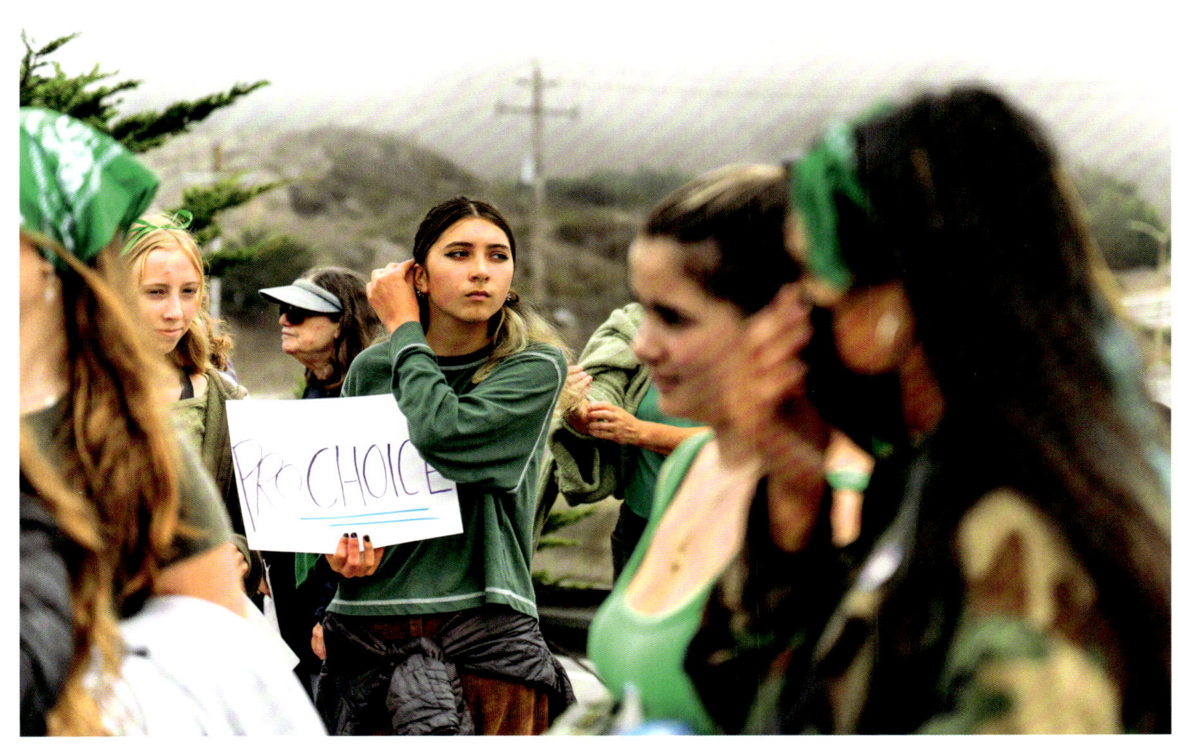

PRO CHOICE

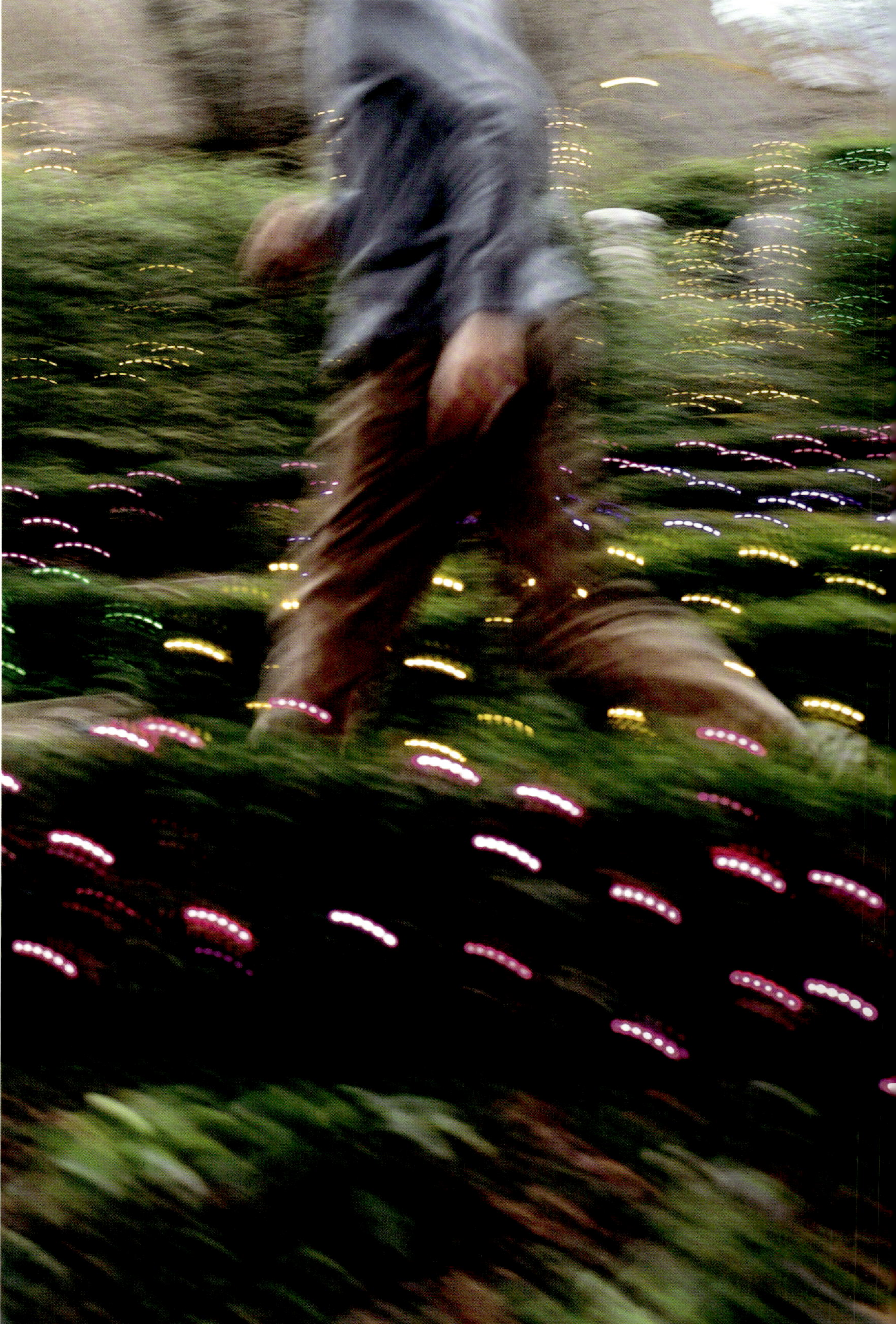

Color is joy. One does
not think joy. One is
carried by it.

—Ernst Haas

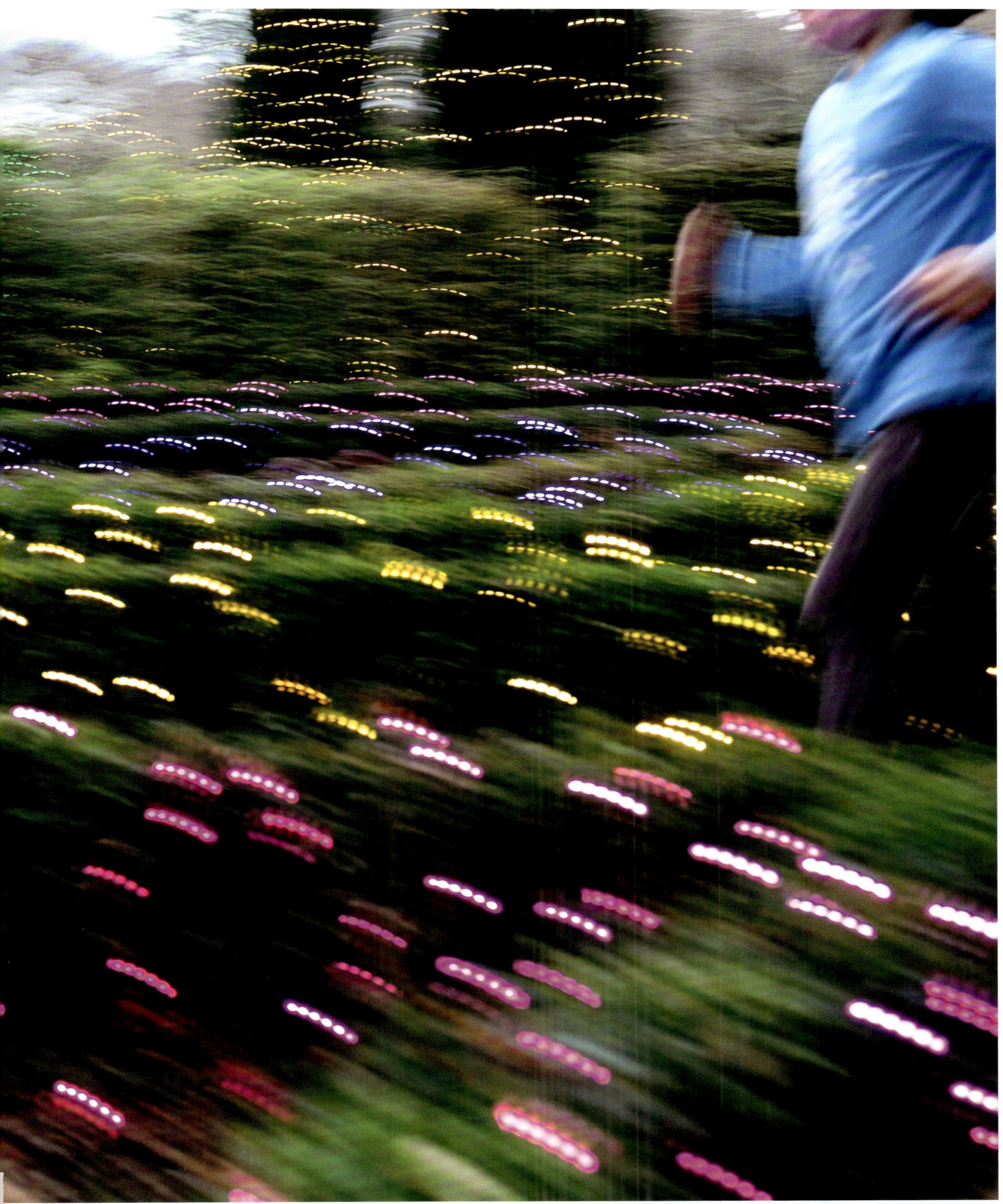

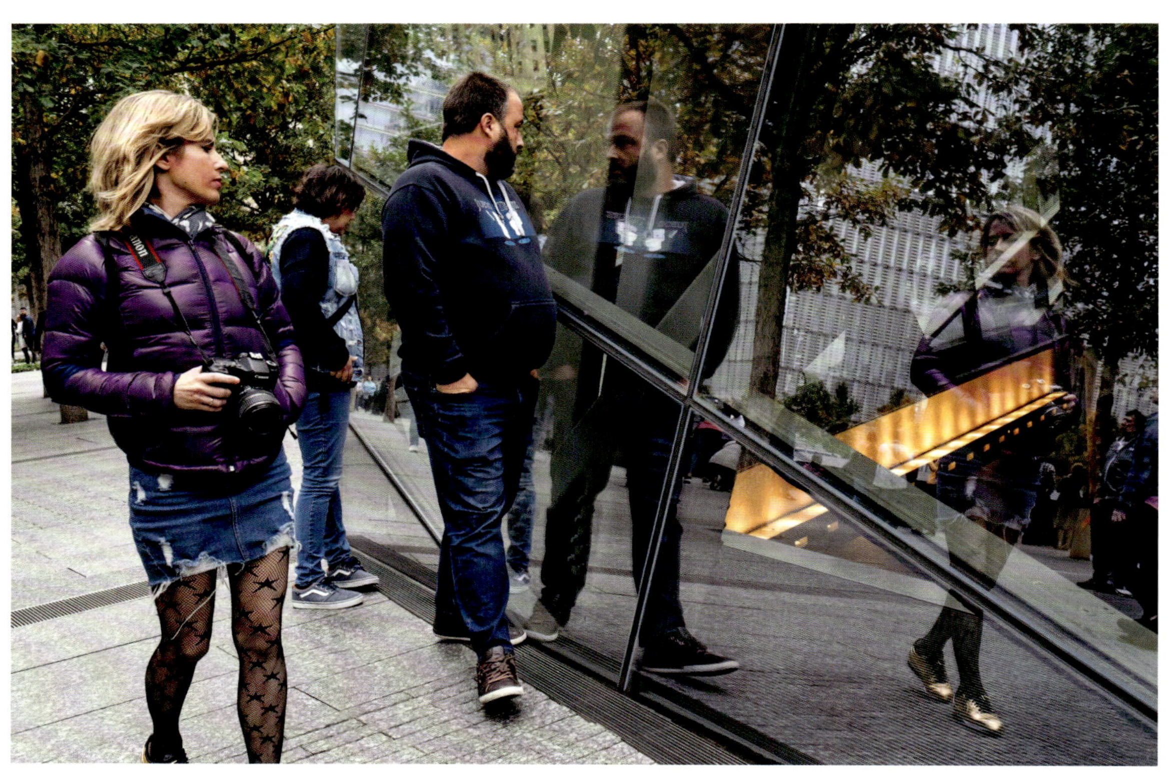

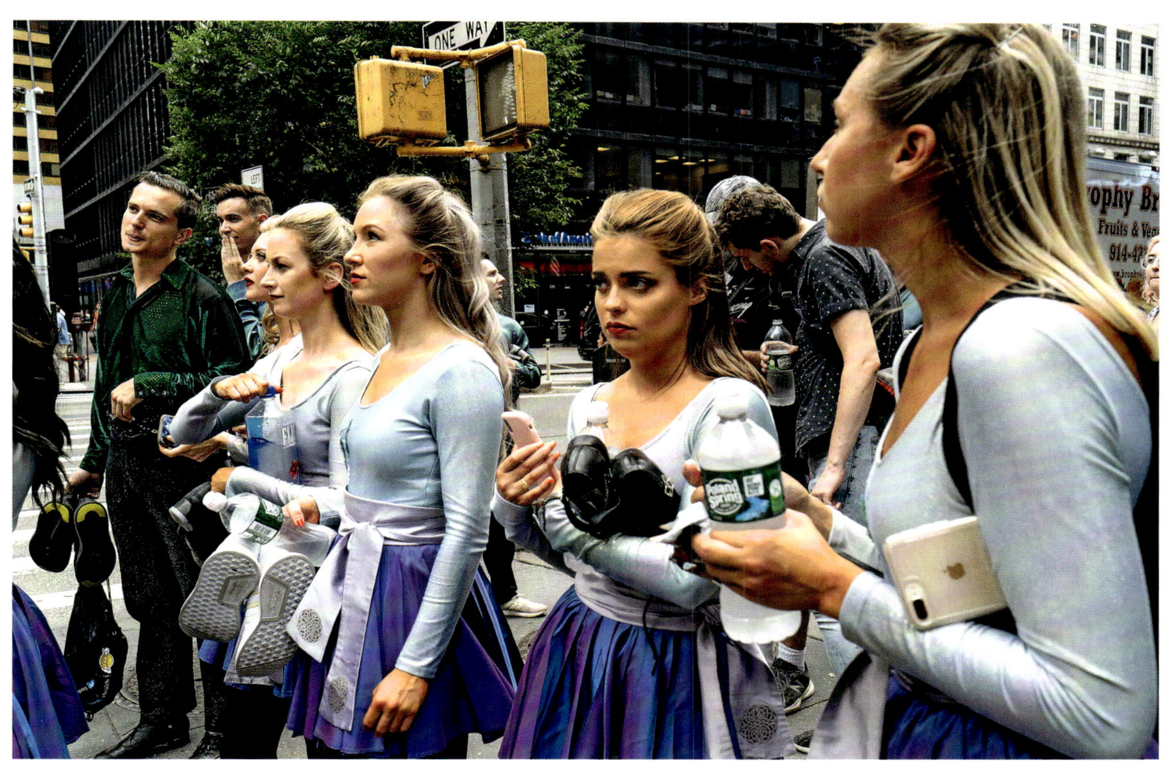

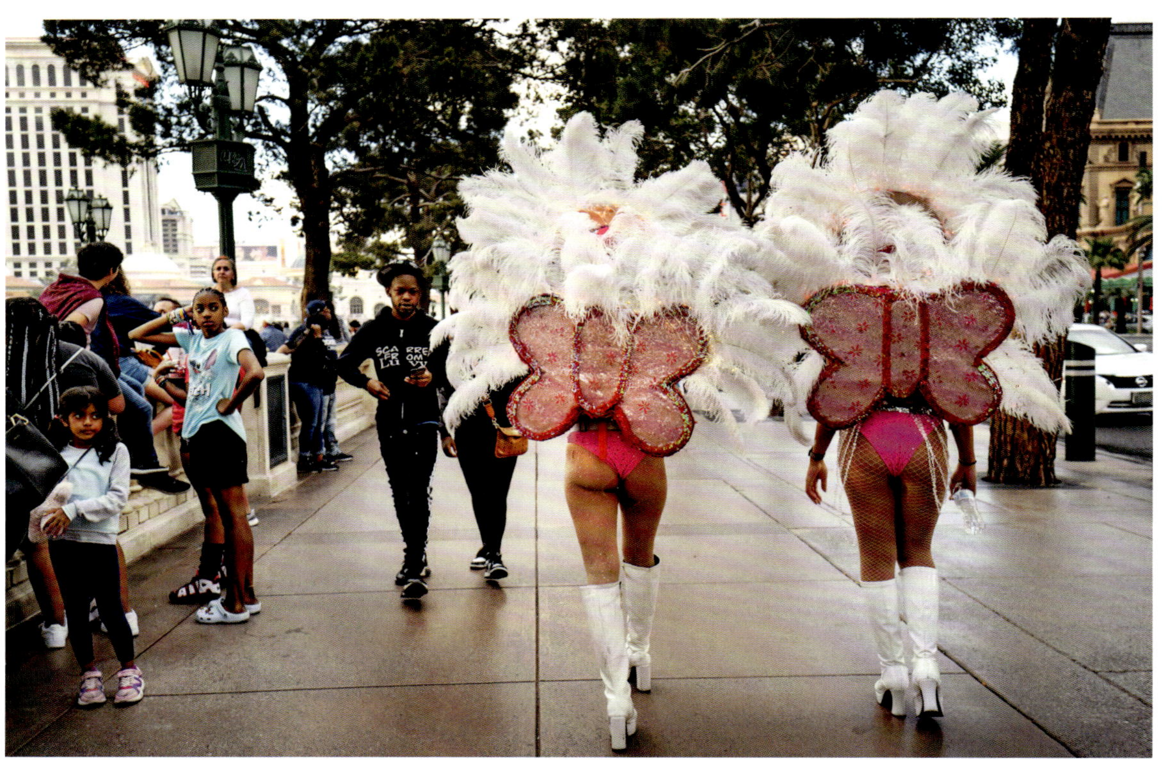

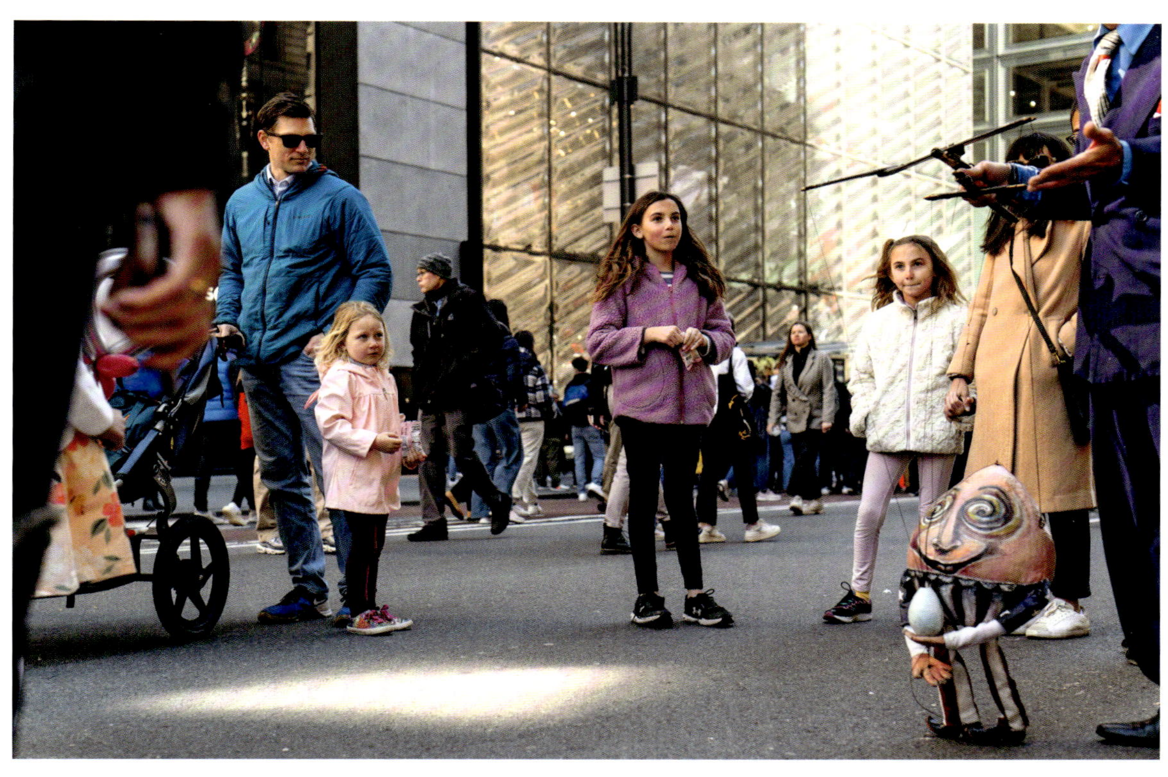

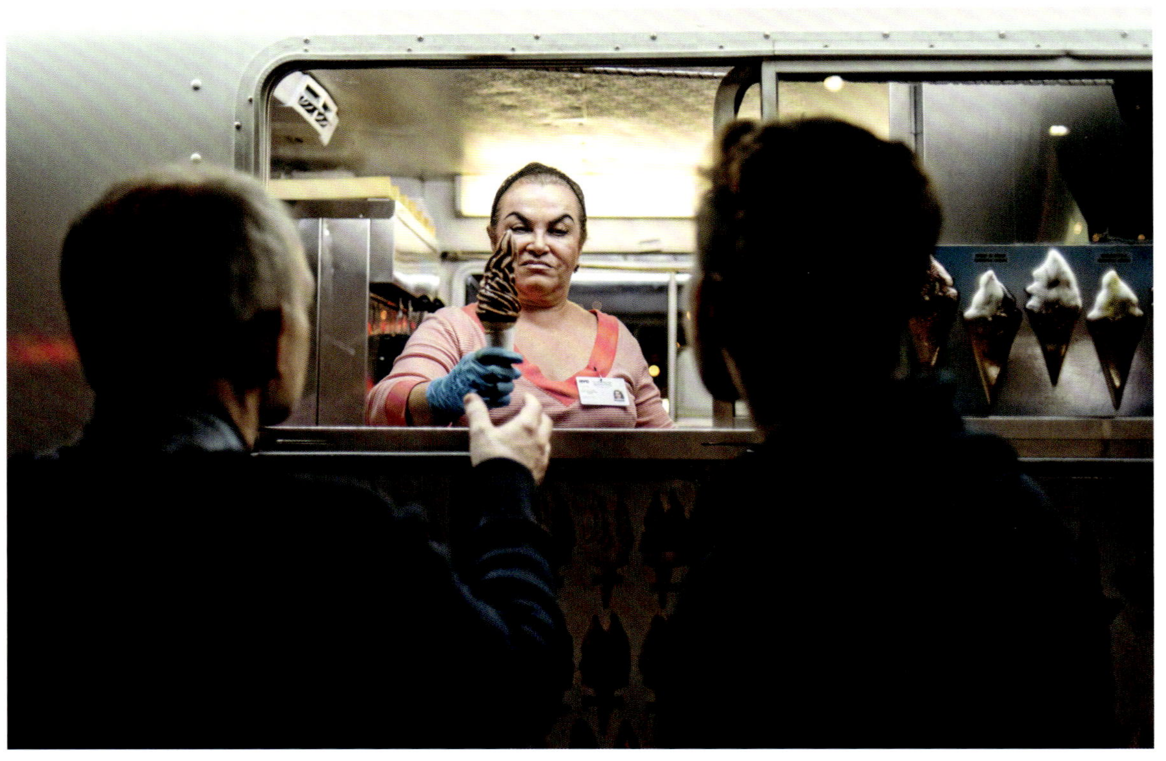

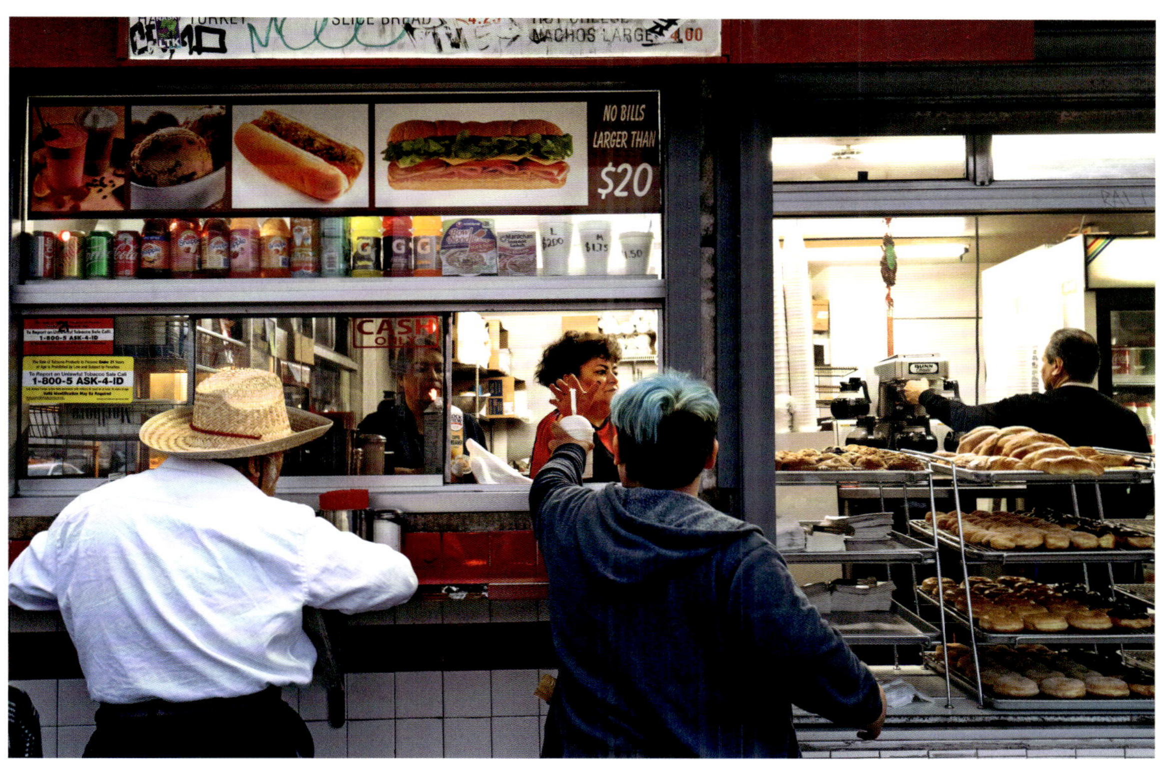
TURKEY
SLICE BREAD
HOT CHEESE
NACHOS LARGE
NO BILLS
LARGER THAN
$20
CASH
ONLY
To Report an Illegal Tobacco Sale Call:
1-800-5 ASK-4-ID
To Report an Unlawful Tobacco Sale Call
1-800-5 ASK-4-ID

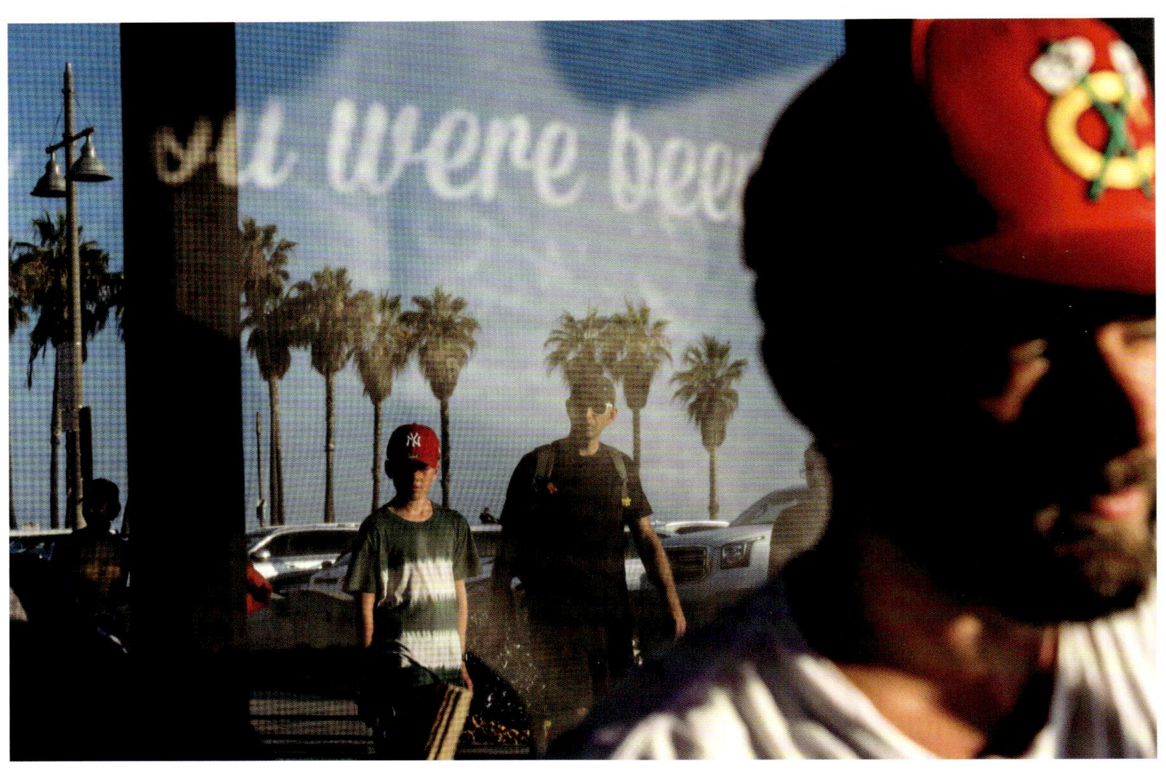
u were beer

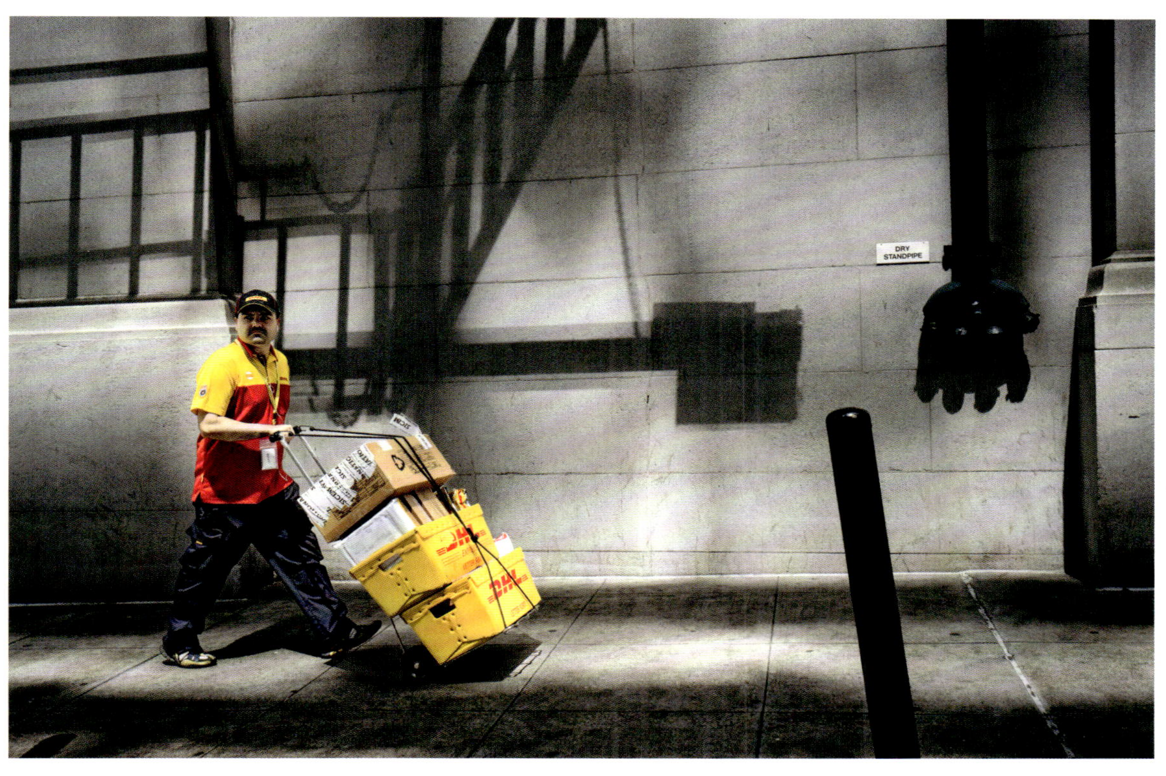
DRY
STANDPIPE
DHL

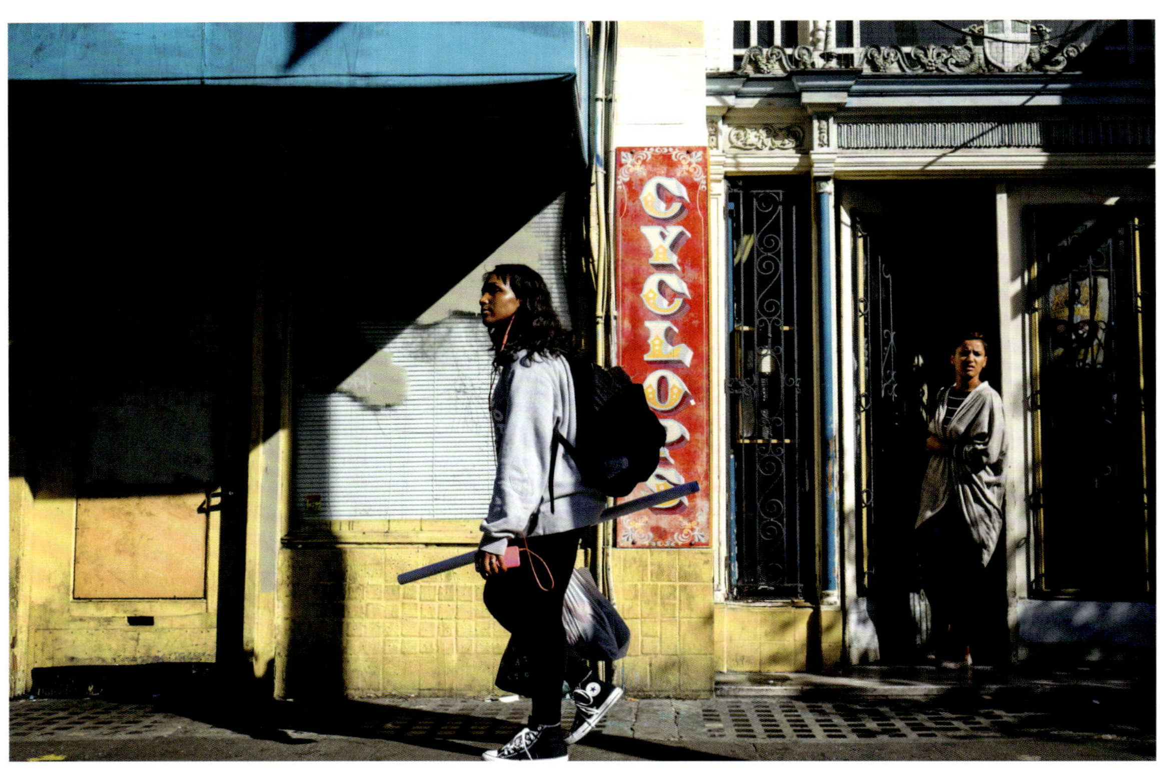

CYCLONE

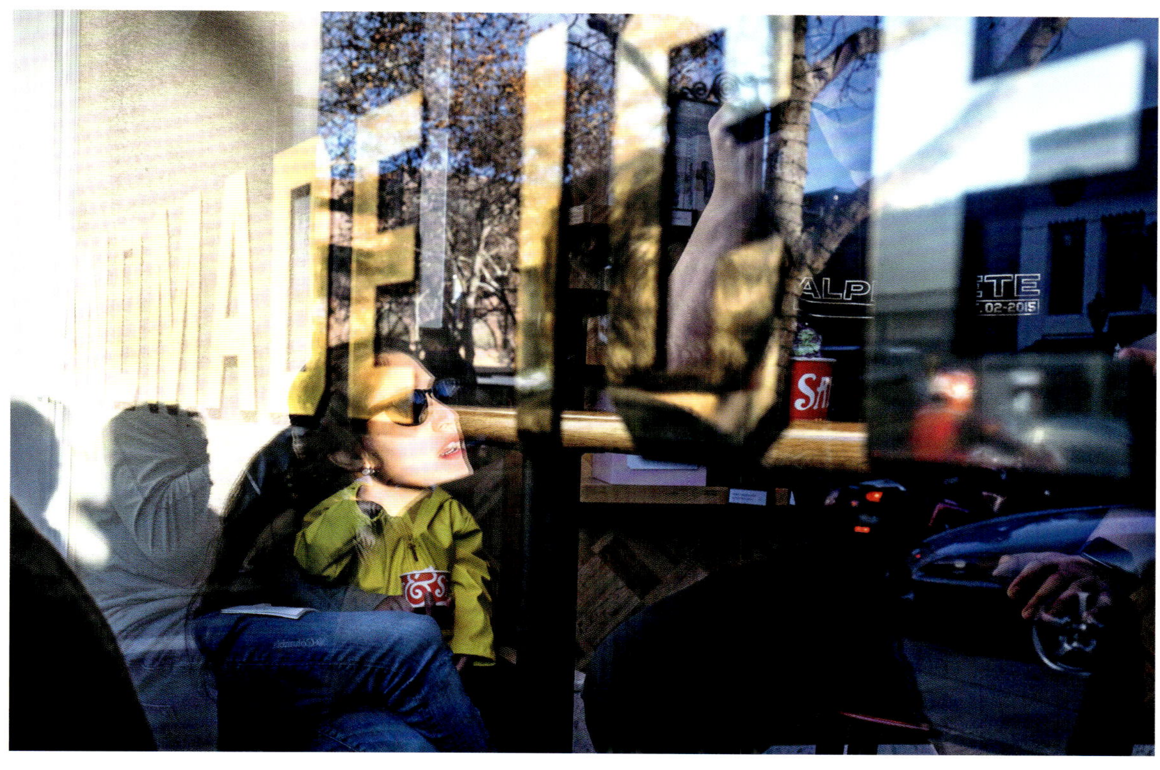

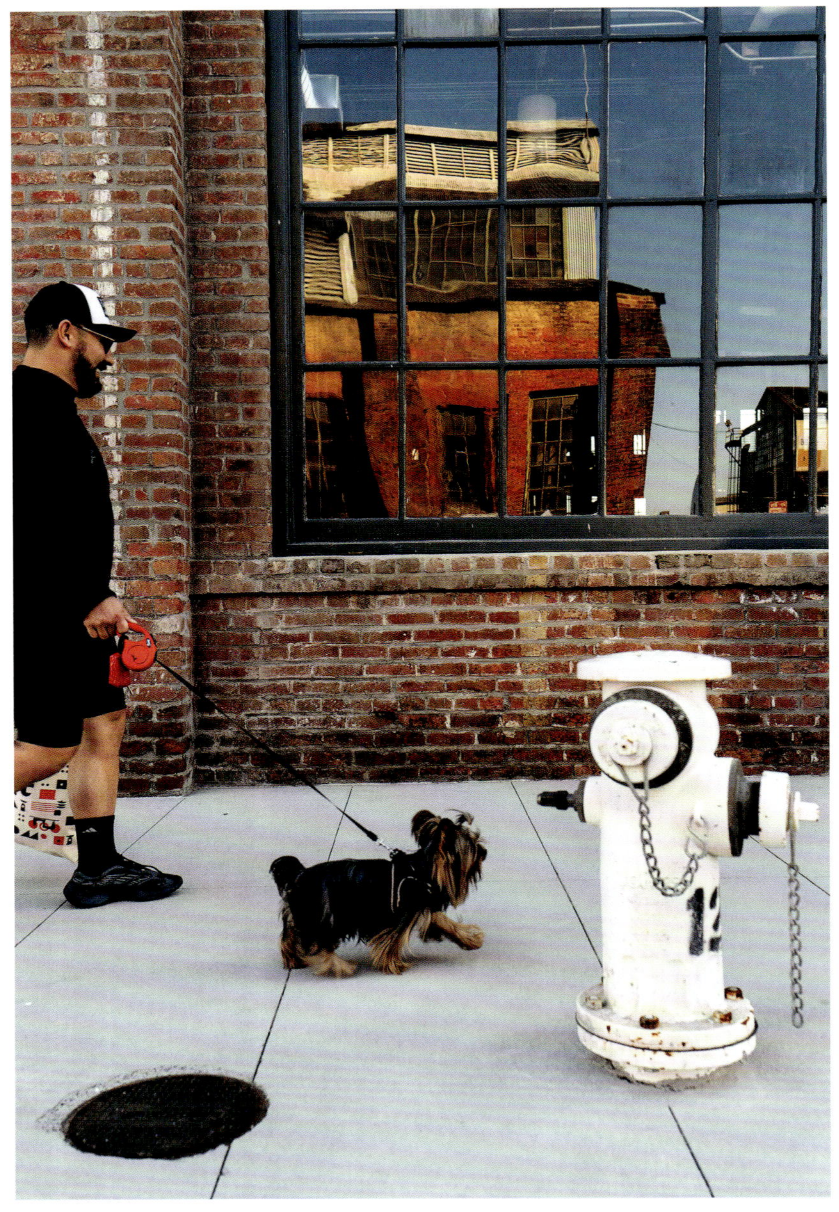

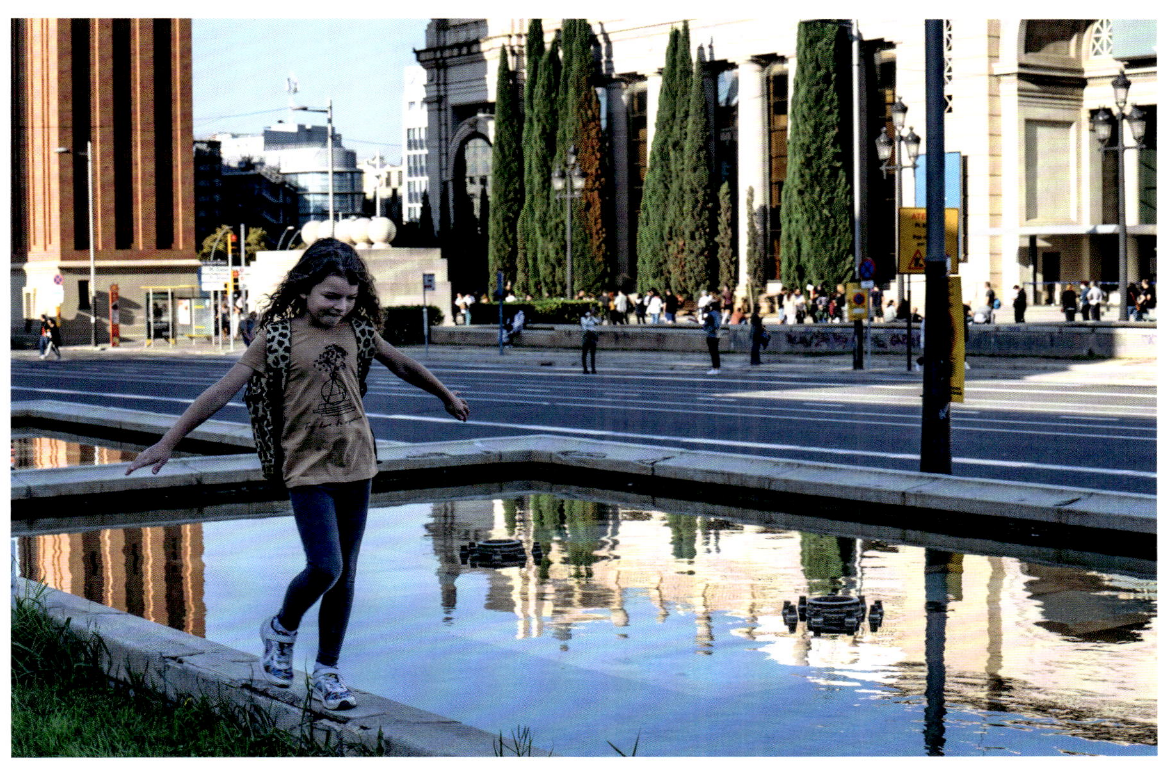

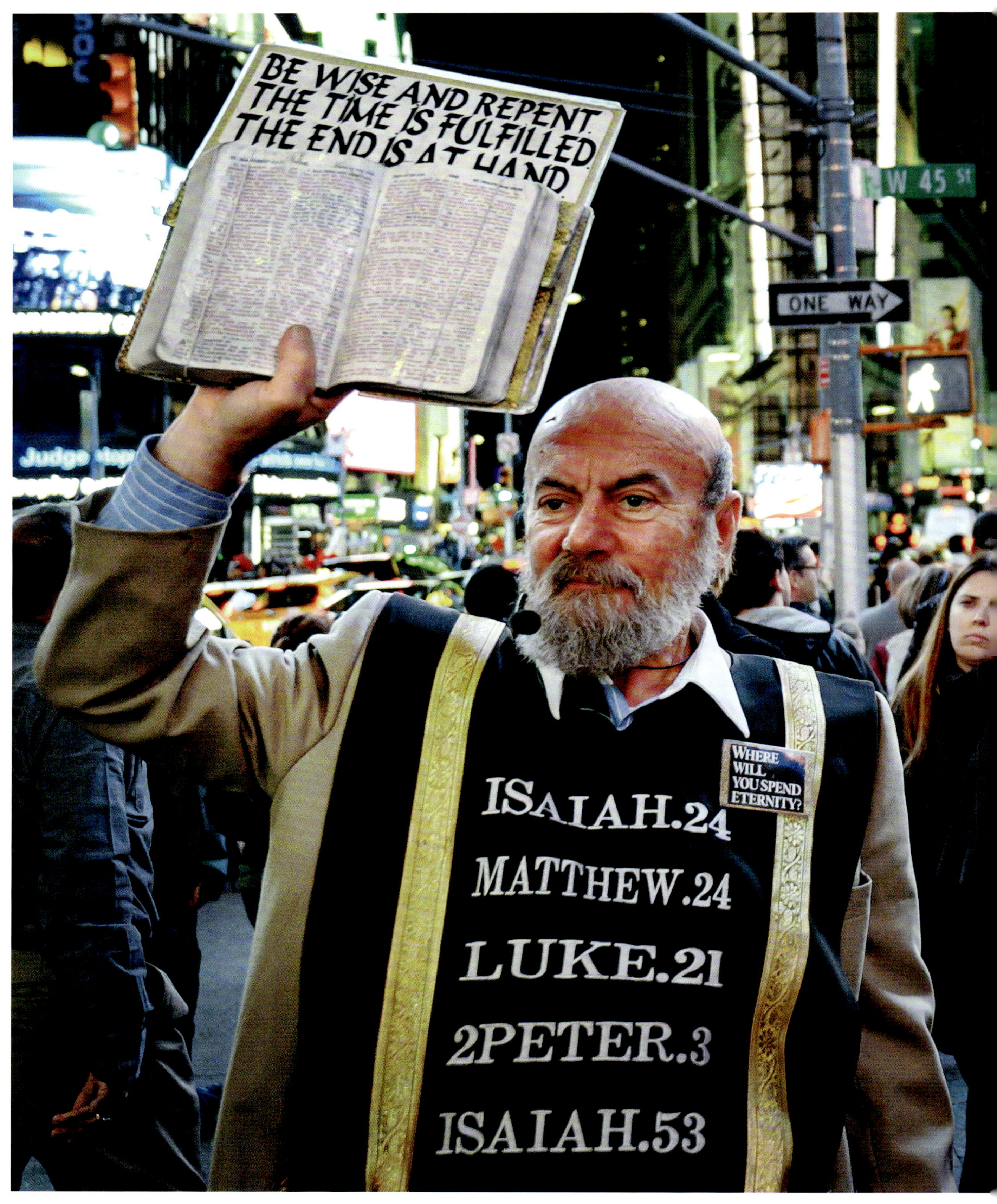

BE WISE AND REPENT.
THE TIME IS FULFILLED
THE END IS AT HAND.
W 45 St
ONE WAY
WHERE WILL YOU SPEND ETERNITY?
ISAIAH.24
MATTHEW.24
LUKE.21
2PETER.3
ISAIAH.53

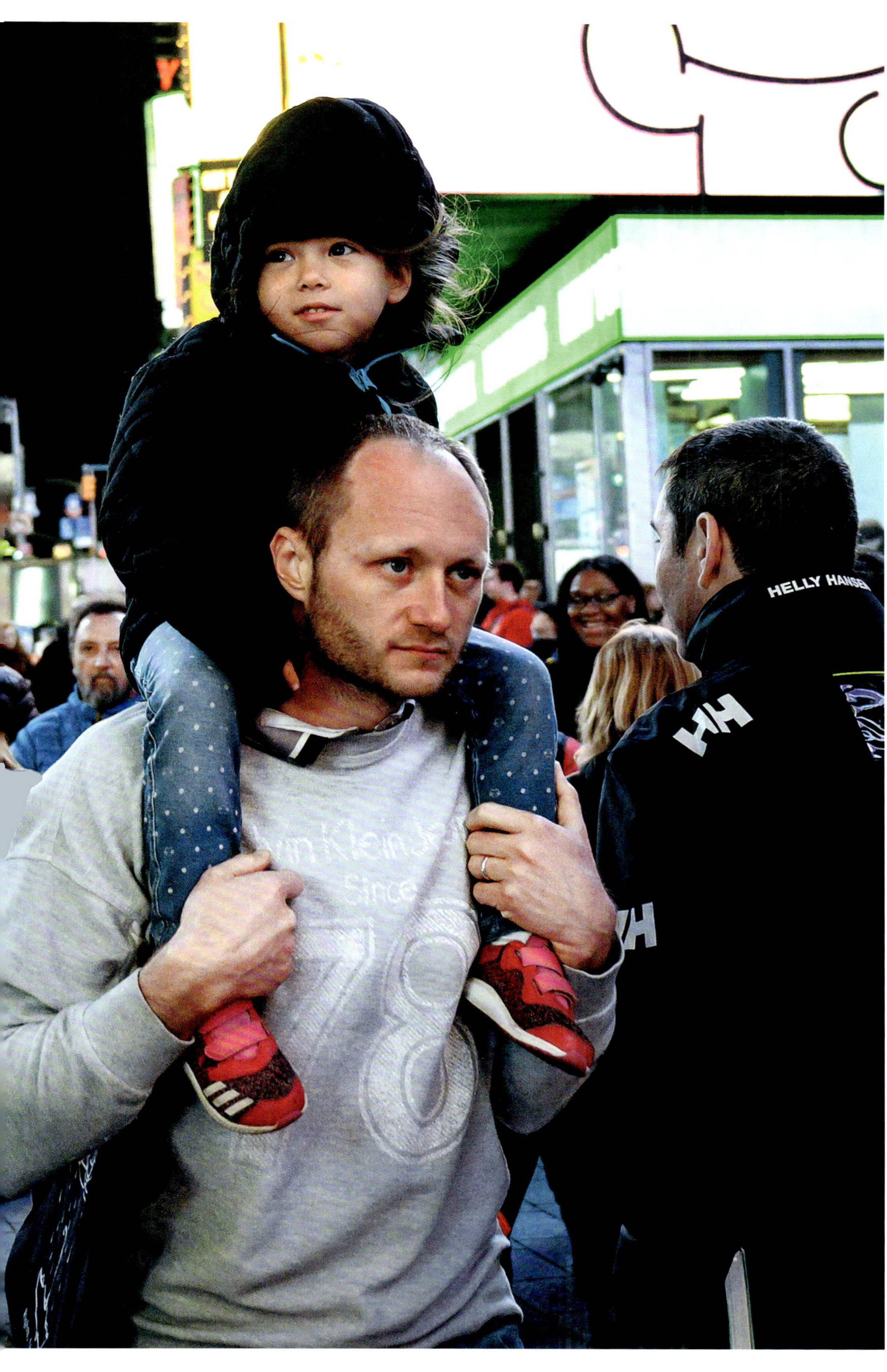

The whole point of taking pictures is so that you don't have to explain things with words.

—Elliott Erwitt

PLATE LIST

AFTERWORD

BY TERI VERSHEL

The photographic community is like a little village. Everyone seems to know everyone and it's a very supportive group. When shooting in Hollywood in 2017, I bumped into a photographer coming out of Musso & Frank, an iconic restaurant on Hollywood Boulevard. We both had Nikon cameras around our necks and got to talking for a minute about photography. I told him I was a street photographer and was roaming the area for inspiration. He told me that he was in Los Angeles for a retrospective of his work and then said, "You've probably never heard of me, but I'm Jay Maisel." I was incredulous, because of course I had heard of him!

I am constantly studying photographs and books from people in the annals of street photography, of whom Jay is an esteemed one. Six years later, when I emailed Mr. Maisel to ask him if I could use a quote attributed to him on the internet in my upcoming book, he picked up his phone in New York and called me in California to tell me emphatically that the quote was not his, but should be properly attributed to Ernst Haas (and then he preceded to give me the exact quote). Getting a random call from Jay Maisel first thing in the morning certainly made my day, but the truly serendipitous part is that Ernst Haas is one of my favorite photographers, and his book *New York in Color 1952–1962* is part of the inspiration for this book. Haas's book is often open in my office, and the photographic pairings are a delight.

In 2018, I met Fred Lyon when he presented his work at a photography exhibit at Pacific Art League in my hometown. He lived in San Francisco his entire life, and his iconic photographs of the city are an inspiration to me. Later, when I called Mr. Lyon and asked if it might be possible for me to come to his studio to pick out one of his photos as a gift for the director of PAL, Fred welcomed me with open arms and proceeded to show me many of his photographic works and discuss several of his books. He even allowed me to take his photo sitting next to a huge print one of his favorite photos, *After Hours Jam, Monterey Jazz Festival*. It was an inspiring day and another example of how the photography community has been warmly encouraging of newer photographers like me.

During the Covid lockdown of 2020, when shooting on the street was not feasible, I decided to make my own book of photographic pairings. I sorted through my archive looking for images that might work well when presented next to each other. As I looked, I found many similarities in gestures and geometry, colors and quality of light. It struck me that, while the people in my photographs are strangers, by comparison they are often related.

ACKNOWLEDGMENTS

I would like to thank my husband, Mark Vershel, for his unending support of my passion and his excellent eye and exacting feedback when asked for editing help. He graciously gave his opinion repeatedly, without being attached to it, and continually encouraged me to trust my instincts. I am grateful to have him in my corner.

Over the years, I have taken many courses on photography. My journey started in the Foothill College Photography program. I would like to thank several instructors whose passion for the medium was contagious. I had my first bookmaking class with Kate Jordahl and I was hooked. I learned about documentary photography from the always lively lectures of Judy Walgren. Finally, thanks to Keith Lee, whose studio lighting classes taught me not only how to properly light a subject, but also that photographing people was really where my heart was.

The workshops I have taken through organizations such as Los Angeles Center for Photography and Santa Fe Workshops have connected me with many professionals in the field and many students with whom I keep in contact. All workshop teachers deserve huge thanks for sharing their passion and taking the time to help all of us grow. The masterful teacher Sam Abell taught me, among many other gems, to compose by waiting patiently and not giving up on a scene too soon. I also owe Mr. Abell many thanks for writing the foreword in this book.

From 2020 to 2021, during the Covid lockdown, I attended many Zoom classes that helped me hone my skills. Through George Nobechi's wonderful Evenings with the Masters series, I met Laura Valenti. My thanks to Laura, as her classes have helped me overcome many photographic roadblocks and taught me to be true to myself and my practice. Special thanks go to Elizabeth Avedon, whose bookmaking class opened my eyes to the possibility of making this book, and whose encouragement and advice was the impetus to try and get it published. Lastly, I would like to thank Ursula Damm, creative director of Daylight, for graciously sharing her extensive bookmaking expertise with me.